HOW TO WIN TO CHRIST

P. E. Burroughs, D.D.

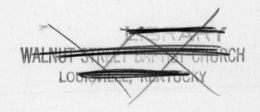
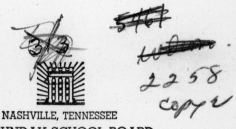

NASHVILLE, TENNESSEE
THE SUNDAY SCHOOL BOARD
of the
SOUTHERN BAPTIST CONVENTION

Printed in the United States of America.
1500—2-39—3

FOREWORD

This book is written and offered primarily for use in the Training Course for Sunday School Workers provided by the Sunday School Board of the Southern Baptist Convention. We seek to offer in this Course carefully-prepared handbooks which will guide and stimulate workers in the Sunday school.

The Course, together with the conditions proposed for its study, is provided for a widely-varying constituency. The books may be offered as texts in colleges and seminaries; they will be studied most largely by busy workers whose minds are occupied with the cares of life. In the effort to meet these varied needs, optional books are offered throughout. In general no specific books in the Course are required for any award, alternate books and choices being everywhere provided.

The helps and directions for study are proposed primarily for busy workers. When the books are offered in educational institutions and under other conditions which justify and demand higher standards, such higher standards will of course be observed.

DIRECTIONS FOR THE STUDY OF THIS BOOK

I. *When the Work is Done in Class*

  1. At least ten class periods, forty-five minutes in the clear, shall be offered

  2. Those desiring awards shall—

    (1) Attend at least seven class periods

    (2) Take a written examination making a minimum grade of seventy per cent, and

    (3) Certify that they have carefully read the textbook.

When it seems impracticable to meet these requirements class members will do the writing required of individual students and send in their manuscripts.

The class teacher, on accepting assignment to teach the class, should send for report blanks. These blanks must be filled out, and the above requirements must be fully met before awards can be granted.

The books should be read during class-study. In case this seems impracticable, a pledge to read the book within the next two weeks will be accepted.

II. *When the Work is Done Individually or by Correspondence*

No examination will be required. Students will make choice of the following:

1. Write answers to the questions printed in the book, or

2. Write a development or elaboration of the chapter outlines.

Correspondence students will study the book in their own way. Then with the open book and any other helps available they will write answers to the printed questions, or they will, if they prefer, write a development or elaboration of the chapter outlines. In either case the students will find it necessary to study the book carefully, to rethink its message and state in their own language its essential teachings.

Written work done by such students will be sent to the Educational Department of the Baptist Sunday School Board, Nashville, Tennessee.

P. E. Burroughs,
Educational Secretary.

CONTENTS

I

WHAT WE PROPOSE AND WHY

I. WHAT WE PROPOSE

It has not been easy to find a suitable designation for these studies. Many phrases have suggested themselves. A brief glance at these phrases, with a statement of the reason why some were rejected and why *How to Win to Christ* was chosen, will indicate the scope of study which we propose.

1. *Evangelism* has, of course, been considered. Strictly speaking, evangelism means winning to Christ by a proclamation of the evangel, the good news of the Christ. It carries the idea of the simple process of bringing to Christ; it speaks of the glorious work of bringing to discipleship, of the initial bringing into the Kingdom of Grace. It can hardly be said to embrace the preparatory processes which are essential to an early and full surrender to Christ, as it does not include the later measures of training and culture which are essential to the rounded completeness of Christian life and character.

The phrase does not seem to serve our purpose for the reason that we wish to include a study both of the preparatory steps and of the later processes of care and culture. Certainly, conversion, the initial coming to Christ, is a central and vital point, but we wish to consider also the influences and training which pave the way for conversion, together with the after-experiences and the training which go to make possible the best fruits of conversion. In a word, we would study the whole rounded process of winning to Christ. We aspire to win to Christ the whole nature with all of its powers and possibilities. While the phrase "Evangelism" is hardly adequate to set forth the purpose of our present studies, yet the word is so significant and so widely used, and that for which it stands so strikes at the heart of what we desire, we shall find ourselves frequently employing it.

2. *Sunday school Evangelism* was proposed. Assuming that the scope of the phrase "Evangelism" is expanded to include the preparatory processes which pave the way for surrender to Christ and the succeeding measures which make for fruitful Christian living, why should not our studies be called "Sunday school Evangelism"?

The Sunday school certainly has come to hold an enlarged place in all winning and life-making efforts. We would emphasize and magnify that place in all proper ways. But we require here a right perspective, giving to all agencies and elements proper place and due emphasis. Apart from the personal element which must always loom large, there are three divinely-given agencies upon which we must chiefly rely—the home, the teaching service, and the preaching service.

Normally, *the home* is the mightiest factor. It has the child in the early, plastic years almost exclusively. Its silent and persistent influence is all but irresistible. It is for the home to give the earliest bent and bias toward God. The influence of a Christian father and mother may count for more toward conversion than all teachers and schools, all preachers and churches; more than all other individuals or institutions. *The church school* further plants the seed of the gospel. Touching the home on one side, it supplements its instructions and appeals; touching the preaching service on the other side, it seeks to win and prepare the life for the service of Christ and his church. Finally, *the preaching service* comes in with its glorious word of atonement and its message of life in Jesus, and reaps in salvation and abundant life the harvest which has been prepared in the work of the home and the Sunday school.

Certainly it is possible to conceive of conversion with one or another of these influences lacking. Men are

saved who receive no Christian impress in the home; men
are converted who never knew the blessing of the Sunday
school; men are sometimes brought to Christ when other
influences than the preaching service seem to operate for
their salvation. But we cannot "win to Christ" in the
best and largest sense without the co-operation of these
three agencies. It is of course possible to bring to a
decision for Christ in the home or in the Sunday school—
even so, it seems good to let the home and the Sunday
school stand in line as contributing and preparatory
agencies and to bring the lost to a confession of Jesus as
Saviour and Lord in the fine atmosphere of the morning
or evening worship, when the whole congregation is gathered before the Lord. So it falls out that while we propose to magnify the Sunday school and give it due
emphasis in this work, yet *Sunday School Evangelism*
seems hardly adequate to set forth our real task.

The Sunday school will best fulfil its mission by doing
team-work with the home on the one hand and the
preaching service on the other hand. The superintendent
and the teachers will do well to count their efforts as
links in a golden chain which is to bring and bind to God.
They must magnify the home, exalting the parents and
supplementing their efforts in all proper ways; they must
also dignify the preaching service and magnify its blessed
ministry. Not the teaching service alone is sufficient in
itself, but the Sunday school doing team-work with the
home and the preaching service is to be mighty and is
to prevail.

3. *Educational Evangelism* was proposed as a possible
designation for these studies. Here again we need to
regard the larger perspective and to preserve a proper
relative emphasis.

Two elements are essential in soul-winning efforts;
education and the evangelistic appeal. When a soul
surrenders to Christ in a blessed experience of grace,
such surrender comes through a twofold process, educational preparation and the revival influence. The education to which we refer may be imparted in an endless

variety of ways; it may be by passive influence or by active teaching; or, better, by both of these. It is safe to say that no soul ever comes to Christ without some such preparation, and in the light of Scripture example and precept it is safe to insist upon the place and meaning of the educational element. It is further true that no soul can come to Christ save through the revival influence. As with education, so with the revival; it may come in a variety of forms and with various manifestations. The revival may or may not involve a protracted meeting. Whenever and wherever a soul is saved, there is a revival, a revival effort, a revival atmosphere, a revival fruit. *"Educational Eangelism,"* as emphasizing the necessary educational processes in soul-winning, is well enough. But if educational evangelism is to obscure the revival element and to eclipse the special and glorious work of the Holy Spirit in regeneration, it becomes a delusion, offering a stone instead of bread.

Because *"Educational Evangelism"* seems to give scant emphasis to the special evangelistic element, the high and mighty work of grace in the heart by which the soul that is dead is made to live, it was not quite acceptable as describing our task.

4. *Child Evangelism.* So far as distinction may be properly made, we wish to approach evangelism from the viewpoint of the child rather than from that of the adult. Such approach seems natural and normal. At the same time we must insist that in its essentials, in its final analysis, child evangelism is not different from adult evangelism. Some one has said, "The New Testament is a book dealing almost entirely with adults." Rather let us say that the New Testament deals with man as man, without regard to age or condition. It is universal in its message and scope. The conditions precedent to baptism are such as are suitable and inevitable for all who come to baptism.

A while ago only adult conversion was believed in or sought, and it was scarcely believed that a child could be saved. The word to children seemed to be, "Except ye be converted *and become as grown men* ye cannot enter the kingdom of heaven." Little effort was made for the conversion of children, and a widespread skepticism existed as to the genuineness of child conversion. Now the pendulum has swung back the other way. Everybody believes in the possibility and necessity of child conversion, while some have almost come to question whether we can any longer win men and women. An eminent minister said a while ago, "In my early days there seemed to be a question as to whether children could be really converted; now there seems to be some question as to whether anybody besides children can be converted." It is well to remind ourselves that the same Lord who took little children in his arms and blessed them also came to seek and to save that which was lost, that he gathered about him publicans and sinners, giving himself and delivering his message to sinful men. Only by deserting the method of the Master can we give the conversion of mature men, yes, of hardened sinners, a secondary place in our expectations and Christian efforts.

The conversion of a child may differ widely from the conversion of a man, as the conversion of a given man may differ widely from the conversion of another man. The experience of a child is usually different from that of an adult in the depth of feeling and in many other particulars, but we do well to lay it to heart that the essentials are in either case the same. Our Lord did not make two atonements, one for the child and another for the man. There were not wrought out two plans of salvation, one for the child and one for the adult. There are not two processes by which we are to come into the kingdom of God, one for children and one for mature people. Insidious peril lurks in the tendency to regard *child* evangelism as an essentially distinct type of evangelism, and to consider the child as somehow possessing inherent innocence which, if it does not make conversion unnecessary, yet makes salvation possible to the child on some easier basis than to the adult.

The Scriptures bring us the conditions of salvation with no hint of distinction between child and adult or between man and man. "There is no difference: for all have sinned, and come short of the glory of God" (Romans 3: 22, 23). "But as many as *received* him, to them gave he power to become the sons of God, even to them that believe on his name" (John 1: 12).

Child evangelism, as indicating and magnifying the winning of children is well enough, but *child evangelism* as hinting that the need and experience of the child is in any essential different from the need and experience of the adult is not for a moment to be accepted. We will approach the great question of how to win to Christ from its normal and natural viewpoint, that of the child in unfolding life, but we will demand and expect conviction for sin, repentance and faith, regeneration; in a word, all the constituent elements which enter into any experience of grace.

5. *Soul-winning* was considered. This phrase is widely used and is deeply suggestive.

Certainly, it may be said that we are concerned to save *lives,* not simply to save *souls;* our commission is to deal with the whole man, the man physically and mentally, no less than the man spiritually. The gospel is not meant alone to cure ills and aches of the heart and wounds of the soul, but to sweeten and save the whole man. It is not simply an insurance agency by which we are to be guaranteed immunity in death and safety in eternity. It is not merely a transportation medium by which we are to have safe transfer from this life to realms of bliss. Our gospel proposes to save men, to save the whole man, here, in time, and this to the end that he may be saved in eternity.

Yet we may not forget that the gospel in saving men deals primarily with sin and concerns itself first of all with the soul. It will sweeten and bless the whole life by

cleansing the inward man from sin. It deals primarily
with the soul, the spirit, where sin dwells and whence
are the fountains of life. True, it is not merely an insurance against loss at death, but it is such insurance. It
is not simply an agency for safe transfer to heaven when
this life ends; yet it is such an agency. Successful evangelism is always based on the conviction that the gospel
saves in the crisis of death and the judgment, that it
gives sure entrance into the presence of God.

If we will purify and sweeten the life we must first see
that the soul, the deep inward source of life, is purified
and sweetened. Sin in the soul is the source of all the
real ills of life. The gospel deals primarily with sin and
begins by saving the soul. "The soul of all improvement
is the improvement of the soul." While the phrase,
"soul-winning," seemed hardly adequate to set forth the
whole work of the Christ in the life and hence hardly
sufficient to describe our present task, it yet strikes at
the heart of that work.

6. Why did we adopt *How to Win to Christ?* Because
this phrase expresses our full-rounded task. It really includes all that is essential in the phrases which we have
presented; it includes evangelism and culture, education
and the revival, soul-winning and all that accompanies
soul-winning. Our real task is to win to Christ, to win
and save the whole life through atoning grace, to redeem
the whole being, all its elements and powers from sin to
the kingdom and service of God. This phrase faces out
toward all life, toward the child and the adult alike; it
includes all that is essential and likewise excludes all that
is non-essential.

"Win" is a strong scriptural word. It implies what
must never be obscured or forgot—that we are by nature
alienated from God, that we must be won back to God.
"He that winneth souls is wise" (Proverbs 11: 30).
The word here used is suggestive; it is taken from the
hunter's craft and literally means "ensnareth," "taketh
alive." Sinful souls, alienated from God, must be en-

snared, taken alive, and delivered back to God. This is winning to Christ.

We have adopted this subject, How to Win to Christ, as the best possible designation for these studies because it fully describes our complete task, which is evangelism, together with its preceding processes of preparation and its succeeding measures of training.

II. WHY STUDY HOW TO WIN TO CHRIST

1. *The task of winning to Christ is supreme and it is supremely glorious.* We are saved in order that we may save. We are chosen and redeemed that we may win others to love the great Saviour and to know the great salvation. The supreme end of every Christian life is somehow, somewhere, to fit into God's mighty plan to save men. Not only is winning to Christ supreme in individual life; it is pre-eminent in the mission of the churches of the Lord Jesus. Each particular church is set in the kingdom for the winning of lost men. In the broad sense in which we are using the term, as saving and building, winning to Christ is the one outstanding obligation of every church.

And this work is supremely glorious. It engages the thought and employs the effort of the Triune God; the Father planned it in the councils of eternity; the Son came to the earth and executed the eternal plan; the Holy Spirit applies and carries forward the atoning work of Christ. This work of winning men which thus engages the efforts of the Father, the Son, and the Holy Spirit, also commands the attention and interest of the unfallen angels and the hosts of the redeemed. As the saints and the angels look down upon the earth and view the affairs of men, they are not so much interested in political revolutions, in ebbs and flows in the financial world, or in social upheavals, as they are concerned for God's redemptive work among the sons of men.

2. *Winning to Christ holds central place in the Sunday school.* Beyond all question the supreme business of the

Sunday school is winning to Christ. We do not forget or obscure the necessity of divine grace in the saving of men and in their spiritual growth, when we urge faithful human effort. This is our task; taking the child at the threshold of its life, we are, through the ministry of the Cradle Roll and through the instruction and training of the Beginner and Primary departments, to prepare him for Christ; very early we are, through divine grace, to bring him to a personal surrender to Christ and acceptance of him as Saviour and Lord; then we are to seek to bring his whole life into harmony with God's will and to make him Christian in all the depth and sweetness of that term.

Failing here, we have failed utterly. It is of little avail that our youths shall grow up to know the Bible if they do not come to know by a vital experience the Christ of the Bible. It is of little moment that men shall come to know the frame-work of Bible history if they are not to know the living Spirit which breathes in every part of that history. We have signally failed if, having taught our youths the Ten Commandments of God, we do not bring them to know and obey the God of the Ten Commandments; if, having taught them to know the Twelve Apostles of our Lord, we do not bring them to know our Lord himself. Let all the estates of Israel, let all the forces of the home and the Sunday school set forth this as the supreme goal, that the young life about us shall be redeemed by the blood and brought into complete subjection and conformity to the will of Christ.

We do well as Sunday school workers to face quietly and faithfully the question as to what in the work of the school shall hold first and commanding place in our thinking. We make much of *numbers*. We bend unremitting efforts to enlarge our attendance. This we ought to do; we cannot teach people until we have first reached them. We make much of *organization*. Well we may; order is God's first law and an orderly organization is essential to success. We are, however, to keep a clear eye on our real goal. We seek numbers and organization with a view to soul-culture and evangelism.

A man in Texas invented a cotton-picking machine. It was a notable achievement. Thousands of earnest men had bent their energies to this end and had failed. This man was elated over his success. Certain officials and government experts came to pass on the merits of the new machine. They looked it over, tested it, found it a perfect bit of machinery, wonderful and complete. They had only one fault to find—*it would not pick cotton.* If the Sunday school fails in winning to Christ, it fails in its main business.

3. *The Sunday school holds a chief place in winning to Christ.* We have already seen that the Sunday school is one of three institutions divinely given for this end; we have entered plea that the Sunday school can only realize its highest usefulness by doing team-work, recognizing the home and co-operating with it on the one hand and supplementing the church on the other hand. The Sunday school, holding, as it does, the early plastic years and gathering alike the saved and the lost, thus touching and blessing life literally from the cradle to the grave, must hold a commanding place in winning to Christ.

Sane evangelism comprises two essential elements, (1) education, and (2) the revival, or the evangelistic appeal. These elements are not to be separated from each other. Education, which is not permeated with the spirit of evangelism, is unavailing; revivalism, which does not build upon education and the many processes of preparation, must be likewise worthless. In the language of Dr. L. R. Scarborough, "Let us evangelize our education and educationalize our evangelism."

We would hardly care to say that our day is witnessing a transfer of emphasis from the revival to education. Let us rather say that there is increasing disposition to put emphasis on the processes of education and training which make possible a perennial revival. We are depending on quiet, persistent evangelism more than on special revival efforts. We are drawing our educational processes and our revival efforts closer together. Our educators, pastors, teachers, and parents are becoming their own evangelists. We have perhaps overworked the saying, "one soweth and another reapeth." God's plan is that sowing and reaping shall be simultaneous, that men shall sow with one hand and reap with the other. Seedtime and harvest need not be widely separated. More and more, pastors are coming to be their own evangelists. Teachers and superintendents are coming to be their own revivalists. The workers who sow are at the same time quietly and persistently reaping. The Sunday school is the fruitful evangelistic opportunity.

The evangelism of tomorrow is to find here its mighty field. The Sunday school holds a first place of influence in the incoming tides of child life, while through its advanced departments it is reaching and influencing adult life as no other agency can hope to do. Because the Sunday school is a pre-eminent evangelistic agency and opportunity, Sunday school workers ought to study the principles and methods of evangelism.

4. *Winning to Christ is an art, the finest of the fine arts, which has its own laws and which requires intelligent effort.* If the impression has prevailed that piety and fervor alone are essential, we may without depreciating these prime essentials, insist that no other art more imperatively calls for equipment and skill. It is true that any fervent soul may accomplish wonders here, but that soul might with skill won by training wield a far wider and safer influence in soul-winning. Here as elsewhere in Christian service, even a little instruction, starting aright and giving some guidance as to method and intelligent efforts, must be helpful.

It is impossible to estimate the harm done by untrained and misguided workers. The soul is peculiarly sensitive and impressionable in those days when it seeks through conviction and confession of sin to know its Lord. Error

planted, wrong bias given, in that critical time may bear
an evil harvest in all after-years.

A vision of the meaning of evangelism and an experience of the joys which come from winning the lost would
transform many a Sunday school. Is it difficult to find
among the great numbers of cultivated men and women
in our churches those who will teach and bear the bur-
dens of the Sunday school? Do those who teach lack
joyful and triumphant zeal? Let the fires of evangelism burn, let the community be pervaded by a quiet,
gracious revival, let the workers get a vision of the meaning and matchless dignity of what we are doing, as
these things touch life and destiny, and all will be
changed. "If I had the trumpet of God," said D. L.
Moody, "and could speak to every Sunday school teacher
in America, I would plead with each one to win at least
one soul to Christ each year."

THINK ON THESE THINGS:

Why is the designation, evangelism, unsatisfactory for our studies?
Why is Sunday school evangelism rejected?
What of educational evangelism?
Why not child evangelism?
State the advantages and disadvantages of soul-winning as a
    designation for our studies.
Why how to win to Christ?
Give reasons of your own for a study of this theme.
Of the reasons given by the author, which do you regard as most
    potent?
State briefly what you hope to gain from these studies.

CHAPTER OUTLINE

I. What We Propose
    1. Evangelism
        Hardly adequate to express our task
    2. Sunday School Evangelism
        Not a complete perspective

3. Educational Evangelism
   Hardly sufficient
   May seem to obscure the revival element
4. Child Evangelism
   Seems inadequate
   Wrong implication
5. Soul-winning
   Suggestive, but hardly sufficient
6. How to Win to Christ
   Chosen because both adequate and sufficient; sets forth our complete task and indicates the studies which we propose

II. Why Study How to Win to Christ
1. This task is supreme and supremely glorious
2. The place which winning to Christ holds in the Sunday school
3. The place which the Sunday school holds in winning to Christ
4. Winning to Christ is an art which, having its own laws, requires intelligent effort

II

What is Winning to Christ?

What is winning to Christ? Precisely what do we mean when we speak of winning to Christ?

I. We Answer Negatively

We seek, first, to clear away some possible misconceptions. Here we must turn to the New Testament and use it as our standard guide.

1. *Winning to Christ, then, is not merely inducing people to "quit their meanness."* It is possible, more, it is highly probable that the reader never thought in such terms. And yet this conception of our task is insidious and persistent. It is as mischievous as it is persistent. It says, "We preach *sin;* quit thy meanness and thou shalt be saved." But the New Testament says, "We preach Christ"; "Believe on the Lord Jesus Christ and thou shalt be saved."

Dr. A. H. Strong declares that this urging of people to "quit their meanness" is like plucking bitter apples from a tree and in their place tying good apples with a string. Quitting our meanness will not suffice. Without Christ and evangelism it is forever impossible. Winning the lost is not simply winning people to give up their sins. Doctor Strong points out that, left to themselves, people cannot quit their meanness; and he continues: "It is regeneration or degradation. Regeneration, the beginning of an upward movement by power not man's own; or degradation, the continuance and increase of a downward movement that can end only in ruin. Much is said about the descent of man. I believe in the descent of man, not from the brute, but to the brute. I do not believe that human nature comes from the brute creation, but I am bound to believe that apart from the constraining influences of the Holy Spirit it tends constantly to the brute creation."

2. *Winning to Christ is not primarily leading the lost to "be baptized and join the church."* This type of evangelism seems always to have found advocacy. This substitute for a real winning of the lost gains and maintains popularity because, from the standpoint of the winner, it is easier to preach, and because, from the standpoint of the sinner, it is easier to accept. It is always simpler and easier to take external material steps than to take exacting internal spiritual steps.

But is it not demanded and expected of all people that they shall be baptized and join the church? Our answer must be "yes" and "no." Here again we face the question as to what is to be first. God demands of all men as a first step that they repent and believe the gospel. The initial steps which must always come first are "repentance toward God and faith toward our Lord Jesus Christ." We are to present Jesus as God's lamb slain from the foundation of the world. Our primary demand must be, "Believe on the Lord Jesus Christ."

Winning to Christ, then, is not leading the lost to be baptized and join the church.

3. *Winning the lost is not merely leading the lost to an emotional experience.* New Testament evangelism sought a sound rather than a merely emotional experience. It did not make the emotions a point of departure or a goal of landing.

A well-known evangelist, who enjoyed rather wide popularity and achieved much apparent success, was accustomed to say: "Not all people are gifted with intellect, hence I do not make approach through the mind; not all people seem to have conscience, so I do not make my primary appeal to the conscience; all people have emotions, hence I make my chief and primary appeal to the emotions."

Nowhere did New Testament evangelism make a primary emotional appeal. It went straight to the heart as the center of spiritual life. It appealed to the mind. Through the mind it made appeal to the heart, the conscience and the will, and thus sought to cleanse the life. Consider again the typical appeal of Peter at Pentecost: God sent his Son and approved him by wonders and miracles and signs, but ye rejected him and by wicked hands crucified and slew him. Thus Peter made first a rational appeal to the mind and through this appeal he touched the conscience. As a natural result he stirred the emotions and moved to action.

Now when they heard this, they were pricked in their heart, and said unto Peter and the rest of the apostles, Men and brethren, what shall we do? (Acts 2: 37).

New Testament evangelism did make real appeal to the emotions. Students of psychology are giving ever enlarging emphasis to the fact that the emotions play a basal part in all life decisions and constitute an essential element in all character-building. In the final analysis, we do only that which we want to do. In the conflict of desires we do that which, all things considered, we most desire to do. Without doubt the emotions constitute a powerful factor in determining what we want to do. Christianity as a mere intellectual system, whether historical or philosophical, can never change and uplift human life. Evangelism must concern itself with the emotions and must reach the emotions if it is to reach and cleanse life. But it should not generally make the emotional approach initial or primary.

4. *Winning to Christ is not necessarily leading the lost to an upheaving or cataclysmic experience*. It is impossible to make too much of a religious experience. Without a religious experience, no man can see God. But it is easily possible to overemphasize certain developments in a religious experience. It is possible so to stress certain phases of emotion and feeling in a religious experience

that we may unwittingly obscure the deep essentials in such an experience.

In this connection we may with profit read the simple stately accounts of some conversions recorded in the New Testament.

> And the two disciples heard him speak, and they followed Jesus (John 1: 37).

> The day following Jesus would go forth into Galilee, and findeth Philip, and saith unto him, Follow me (John 1: 43).

Those of course who have "missed the mark" at the point of sin in its more usual acceptance, those who have gone deep into immorality and have in their lives defied God, may have an experience similar to that which came to Saul of Tarsus. Some indeed who have not gone so deep into sin may have such experience. There have always been such experiences and there doubtless will always be such experiences. But such experiences were not especially sought or considered as necessarily typical in New Testament times.

II. WE ANSWER POSITIVELY

Having thus considered winning to Christ in a negative way, we turn to consider, positively, some marks of winning to Christ as they are reflected in New Testament teaching and practice.

1. *New Testament evangelism put the cross of Jesus always at the center.* It offered as the sole hope for a wayward and sinning humanity the sacrificial death of Jesus. Under all conditions and with all people it sounded this note. But, we let the New Testament Scriptures speak for themselves.

> And as Moses lifted up the serpent in the wilderness, even so must the Son of man be lifted up; that whosoever believeth in him should not perish, but have eternal life (John 3: 14, 15).

> And I, if I be lifted up from the earth, will draw all men unto me (John 12: 32).

"Any gospel," says Dr. P. T. Forsyth, "that ignores the cross in its relation to sin is unfit to cope with the actual case of the world, its giant souls and hearty sinners. Without the message of the cross our message is a very lovely song of one that has a pleasant voice and can play well on an instrument. And the people hear and do not. They are enchanted but not changed."

2. *New Testament evangelism led people to enter earnestly into the spirit of Jesus' teachings and to apply his teachings in daily life.* In New Testament times, believers were friends, imitators, followers of Jesus. Men were expected not so much to subscribe to a creed as they were asked to join themselves to the living Christ and to walk with him in his way of living. This was the test which Jesus imposed: "Whosoever heareth these words of mine, and *doeth them*" (Matthew 7: 24). In this connection we may well ponder the words of Jesus to John's disciples: "Go and tell John the *things which ye have seen and heard.*" Christianity in New Testament times was something which could be seen and heard. New Testament evangelism led men to do and be.

3. *New Testament evangelism built upon carefully-laid foundations.* New Testament evangelism sought out, as we shall later see, men and women who were devout and expectant, men and women in whom had been wrought careful preparation. Such were the people to whom Jesus gave himself most largely and on whom he relied to reproduce and extend his own evangelism. That which Paul said to Timothy could have been said with equal propriety of the disciples of Jesus and of practically all his followers who had part in extending the appeal of Christ: "From a child thou hast known the holy scriptures" (2 Timothy 3: 15).

The success and value of any evangelism must depend upon the material upon which it is permitted to operate. A necessary element in evangelism is the preparation which is made for it. A plain country preacher won George W. Truett to Christ. That country preacher was brought to Jesus by A. C. Dixon while he was on a round of pastoral visiting in Asheville, North Carolina. Much has been made of that country preacher, and Mr. Dixon pleasantly claimed to be the "grandfather" of George W. Truett because he had led that preacher to Christ. All honor to the quiet man who won the lad to the Saviour! But what of the praying father and the pious mother who through infancy and childhood had kept the growing youth close to his Heavenly Father and had patiently taught him about the Lord? What of the gentlefolk who as relatives and teachers had sought to press him close against the heart of Jesus? Did these have no part in the evangelism which won the youth to an acceptance of Jesus as Saviour?

We make much, and properly so, of the great step in which one accepts and confesses Christ, but what are we to say of the prolonged preparatory processes which not only lead to that great step, but which largely determine what is to be offered to Christ and his kingdom in the act of accepting Jesus?

4. *New Testament evangelism made much of Christ's churches.* Jesus himself centered his labors on the founding of his church. As he marched toward the cross his church loomed before him. His church was constantly in his thinking. To his church he was to commit his gospel. When Paul and his associates went afield preaching Christ as Saviour and Lord they everywhere established churches. To the churches or for the churches all of the books of the New Testament were written.

In so far as the churches are concerned, evangelism falls into three classes:

(1) There is church evangelism. This is evangelism which is by the church, and through the church and for the church. In a word, it is by the body of Christ, through the body of Christ and for the body of Christ. This evangelism deserves to rank first and highest in all efforts to publish the good tidings. Thus a given church may prepare for Christ, win to Christ and train in Christ.

It is good for the lost to find Christ in Christ's church. This is normal New Testament evangelism.

(2) There is inter-church evangelism. In this type the churches of a community or section join together in the effort to win people to Christ. Manifestly they cannot thus carry through any full program of evangelism; they cannot jointly do the preparatory work, nor can they jointly do the work of nurture and training. They may, for convenience and in order to reach people who might not be reached by local programs, blend their efforts in proclaiming the evangel. There will always be a place and need for this type of winning work.

(3) There is extra-church evangelism. This evangelism is conducted generally by church people, but apart from the churches.

The churches will favor and rejoice in any effort made under any conditions to preach Christ. They are ever ready to say with Paul: "Christ is preached; and I therein do rejoice, yea, and will rejoice."

The most wholesome and the most promising sign on the evangelistic horizon now is the tendency toward church evangelism. As never before in the history of American Christianity, the churches, through their pastors, deacons, teachers, and other workers, are conducting their own programs of winning. In this, they are following the pattern shown us in the New Testament and are reproducing New Testament evangelism. Now abideth church evangelism, inter-church evangelism, and extra-church evangelism, these three; and the greatest of these is church evangelism.

5. *Winning to Christ, whether in the Old Testament or in the New Testament, rested upon certain fundamentals.*

These may be briefly stated as follows:

(1) Some things which God must do:

a. God must provide a sacrificial substitute, a sin-bearer, a mediator, a maker of atonement (at-one-ment).

b. God must work the marvel of the new birth. Jesus stated an essential and ageless truth when he said, "Except a man be born again, he cannot see the kingdom of God" (John 3: 3).

c. God must sanctify; God must carry on to completeness and perfection the work which he begins in the heart.

(2) Some things which man must do:

a. Man must repent; he must see sin in its real nature and turn from it.

b. Man must believe on "the Lamb of God slain from the foundation of the world."

c. Man must persevere in grace; man must "work out" the salvation which God has wrought within.

This condensed tabular statement may well be pondered, elaborated and illustrated by the reader in his own study. It is not complete, but it is comprehensive in that it includes the chief elements in the winning of the lost.

THINK ON THESE THINGS:

Would you wish to add more negative answers to the question, What was New Testament evangelism? If so, indicate them.

Which of the negative answers given to the question do you regard as most important? Why?

Which of the positive answers given do you regard as most vital?

Would you add other positive answers?

Indicate some marks of New Testament evangelism.

In what respects do you think present-day evangelism resembles New Testament evangelism?

In what ways does present-day evangelism seem to you to differ from New Testament evangelism?

Give in Scripture language two or more conversion experiences.

What are the "fundamentals" in all evangelism?

CHAPTER OUTLINE

I. We Answer Negatively
  1. Not merely inducing people to "quit their meanness"
  2. Not leading the lost to "be baptized and join the church"
  3. Not merely leading the lost to an emotional experience
  4. Not necessarily leading to an explosive or cataclysmic experience

II. We Answer Positively

  New Testament Evangelism
  1. Put the cross of Jesus always at the center
  2. Led to accept the teachings of Jesus and apply them in daily life
  3. Built upon carefully-laid foundations
  4. Made much of Christ's churches
  5. Rested upon certain fundamentals

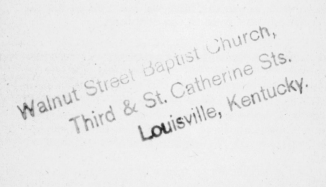

III

QUESTIONS FOR WINNERS AND SINNERS

Men have lost their way; they have wandered from Jehovah. The Bible plea then is that men shall seek Jehovah. This note runs through the Scriptures, both the Old Testament and the New. The Scriptures abundantly answer all questions arising out of this plea. The questions which generally arise are. (1) Why seek God? Why should men concern themselves about God? (2) How seek God? On what conditions is God to be found? (3) When seek God? When the *why* and the *how* of seeking God are settled a final question arises, *when* shall we seek God? The Scriptures answer fully these questions. Since these are precisely the questions which our friends whom we wish to win to Christ will raise, we do well to ponder the answers given in the Scriptures.

I. WHY SEEK GOD?

The Bible as a whole is God's answer to this question. The reasons for seeking God are legion and they are as weighty as they are numerous.

1. *We ought to seek God because God is seeking us.* We ought to concern ourselves about God because God concerns himself about us. We ought to know God because God knows us. We ought to love God because God loves us.

(1) God is seeking us by means of his goodness. God seeks to save us by being good to us. This is the meaning of all the blessings God has given into our lives. God is seeking to win us by being good to us. "If ever the story of your life is written," said Dr. T. DeWitt Talmage, "I will tell you what it will be about; it will be about mercy, the mercy which hovered over your

cradle, the mercy which will hover over your grave, and the mercy which will hover all between the cradle and the grave."

Paul declares this when he asks with a touch of indignation, "Or despisest thou the riches of his goodness and forbearance and longsuffering, not knowing that the goodness of God leadeth thee to repentance?" (Romans 2: 4).

God's goodness leadeth to repentance. God is good to us in order to lead us to repentance. If we refuse thus to be led we then despise the riches of his goodness and forbearance and longsuffering.

(2) God seeks men through severity and reverses. When men despise God's goodness and forbearance and longsuffering, God sometimes turns his goodness into severity. When God cannot win men by his smile, he may turn his smile into a frown. In almost any group of people there will probably be some who could testify that when God through his goodness could not reach and win them, God turned his goodness into severity and won them through trial and reverse.

A pastor sat with a farmer on the lawn of the farm home during a Sunday afternoon. The farmer was a deacon and an exemplary Christian. The two men exchanged their experiences in finding the Lord. The minister related his simple experience and told how as a child he sought and found Jesus as Saviour. When the farmer's turn came he hesitated. "I do not often tell my experience," he began, "I can never tell it without a sense of pain."

Slowly and thoughtfully he went on with his story about as follows:

> I owned this farm, and children came to make our home happy. My wife entreated me to become a Christian, but I delayed. One day when I came in from the farm my wife had an anxious look on her face. "Jack," she said, "Jack, Junior, is sick; I wish you would come in and see him; I am troubled about him."

I went in and examined the lad and saw that he was very sick. I sent for a nurse and called the family doctor. But the boy grew worse. Pastor, do you see that clump of trees out yonder? Well, I went out there and tried to pray. I think it was the first time in my life I ever really tried to pray. But somehow I knew that my prayer was not heard. I came back to the home and my wife said, "The lad is worse." I felt sure that he was not going to get well. He lingered a few hours and then slipped away from us.

When we returned from the long, sad journey to the cemetery, my heart was filled with rebellion. I was tempted to curse God and declare him unjust. I saw other children playing around their homes and my soul cried out against God for taking my boy.

My wife called me in and said, "Jack, I think I understand; I am afraid God is seeking to win you, and because his goodness could not avail, he may have turned his goodness into severity." Her words pierced my heart and right then and there I yielded myself to God.

Such experiences as this are not wholly uncommon. It accords with all that we know of God as a faithful Father to believe that when his gentleness fails to win he may turn his goodness into severity.

(3) God seeks men through his providences. A tragedy occurs in a circle of boys. A member of a group is suddenly removed. A wise teacher may use this providence to make appeal to the group. Every one familiar with the life of Adoniram Judson must recall how when he was far from God and was fighting against all serious impressions, the death of his college mate won him to repentance and confession.

2. *We ought to seek God because we need God*. There must be times when every soul feels its need of God. In every life there must be some aching void. We may seek

to fill that void with pleasure or license. It will not be filled until Christ is formed in us, the hope of glory.

Augustine said what men in all ages have felt: "I was made for thee and I can never find rest until I find it in thee." Dr. Clay I. Hudson tells the story of how Mr. Rudyard Kipling on one of his visits to this country was a guest of the city of San Francisco where he fell ill. The city fathers secured for Mr. Kipling the best physician and the best nurse available and gave the nurse instruction: "Give Mr. Kipling anything he wants, anything that money can buy or science can provide." The distinguished patient was very ill. Far in the night he was trying to speak. The nurse leaned down near to catch his words. She could only hear him say, "I want—" "I want—" The nurse said, "Mr. Kipling, tell me what you want. This city has told me to give you anything that money can buy or that science can provide." She leaned low and eagerly listened. At length she heard the sick man say out of the depths, "I want— "I want *God.*" The man spoke for uncounted millions whose deep persistent cry is, "I want God."

We ought to seek God because we need God.

3. *We ought to seek God because God needs us.* God has a plan for each of us and no other can fit into the plan made for us. It is wonderful, but we may be well assured that it is true; God needs us. He needs our witness; he needs our voice in song. He needs the service which we alone can render. We have already seen how Moses made plea to Hobab saying first, "You need God." When the plea failed, Moses said, "God needs you and Israel needs you." This last plea seems to have won response from Hobab. There are many noble souls to whom this plea will make special and winning appeal.

4. *We ought to seek God because if we seek him he will be found of us.* His every invitation is a guarantee. His every promise is an assurance. God will not invite us and then hide himself from us when we seek him. Noth-

ing can be more sure than that if we seek God he will be found of us.

These, surely, are good reasons why we should seek God; that God is seeking us; that we need God; that God needs us; and that God will be found of us.

II. How SEEK GOD?

If we are satisfied as to the why, if we are minded to seek God, the question naturally arises, "How shall we seek God?"

There can be little difficulty at this point. It cannot be hard for the seeking sinner and the seeking Lord to find each other. We may not be able to make clear to those whom we would win that every impulse to seek God is the creation of God. But we ourselves must know that all desire for God and every wish for God is created by God himself. "Salvation is of the Lord."

1. *We should seek God as any wayward son might seek a neglected and aggrieved father.* It is all simple enough. The prodigal son in his return to his father has been both guide and inspiration for returning sinners. The successive steps will be readily recalled.

(1) The prodigal "began to be in want."

(2) He "came to himself." He had been beside himself. Every sinner wandering from God and rebelling against God is beside himself. *He came to himself.*

(3) He said, "In my father's house is plenty and to spare and I perish with hunger."

(4) He said, "I will arise and go to my father."

(5) "And I will say, Father I have sinned against heaven and in thy sight."

(6) "And he arose and came to his father."

(7) His father "ran to meet him." It is the only time God is ever represented as being in a hurry. When he created the universe he moved by deliberate stages, but when the prodigal was returning he "ran" to meet him.

2. *We should seek God with our whole heart.* The promise is ours: "And if ye seek him, he will be found of you" (2 Chron. 15: 2). When we burn the bridges behind us; when we finally resolve that we will seek the Lord until we find him, then it is that we quickly find him.

3. *We must seek God with a will to forsake every sin and to abandon every evil way.* Our sins stand between us and God. The ringing challenge of John the Baptist and Jesus was "repent"! But repentance means three things: (1) change your mind toward sin; (2) change your feelings toward sin; (3) change your attitude toward sin.

III. When Seek God?

If we are convinced as to the *why* of seeking God; if we are satisfied as to the *how* of seeking God, a final question arises: when shall we seek God? Satan takes here his last stand. He will say when he must, "Yes, you ought to seek God; yes, the way of seeking him is plain enough, but the time—why should you concern yourself to seek God now?

Out of God's Word come these definite suggestions as to when we should seek God.

1. *Men ought to seek God "while he may be found."* This would seem to be reasonable. If we mean to seek God, we ought to seek him while he may be found. There are in the Scriptures definite statements that the time may come when God will not be found of us. We who would win men to seek the Lord may well ponder long and deeply the word of Jehovah as recorded in Proverbs 1: 24-29:

> Because I have called, and ye have refused; I have stretched out my hand, and no man hath regarded;
>
> But ye have set at nought all my counsel, and would none of my reproof;
>
> I also will laugh at your calamity; I will mock when your fear cometh;

When your fear cometh as desolation, and your destruction cometh as a whirlwind; when distress and anguish come upon you.

Then shall they call upon me, but I will not answer; They will seek me early, but they shall not find me;

For that they hated knowledge, and did not choose the fear of the Lord.

2. *Men ought to seek God "early."*

Those that seek me early shall find me (Proverbs 8: 17).

"Early" is literally "diligently"; the diligent seeker will naturally be an early seeker.

Remember thy Creator in the days of thy youth, while the evil days come not, nor the years draw nigh, when thou shalt say, I have no pleasure in them(Ecclesiastes 12: 1).

3. *Men ought to seek God "now."*

God is saying to every lost soul,

Behold, now is the accepted time; behold, now is the day of salvation (2 Corinthians 6: 2).

Whoever would win men to Christ must have a clear and compelling conviction as to the urgent and imperious necessity of seeking God; he must have a sure and full vision of the method of seeking God and he must have a definite and positive desire that men shall seek God without delay. Thus an appreciation of the why of seeking God, an understanding of the how of seeking God, and a conviction as to the time when men should seek God—these are the prerequisites, the conditions, on which we may hope to be winners.

THINK ON THESE THINGS:

Was the Word of God recorded in Isaiah 55: 6 spoken to saints or sinners?

Through which of the means discussed were you brought to seek God?

Which of the reasons given for seeking God seem to you to be the most convincing?

Tell briefly *how* we are to seek God.

Is there a time when God may not be found? Justify your answer from the Scriptures.

What are some advantages in seeking God *early?*

Why should we seek God *now?*

Tell briefly some experience in which you have led some one to seek God.

CHAPTER OUTLINE

I. Why Seek God?

    1. Because God is seeking us

        (1) By his goodness

        (2) Through severity

        (3) Through his providences

    2. Because we need God

    3. Because God needs us

    4. Because he will be found of us

II. How Seek God?

    1. As a wayward son might seek his father

    2. With the whole heart

    3. Willing to forsake every sin

III. When Seek God?

    1. "While he may be found" (Isaiah 55: 6)

    2. "Early" (Proverbs 8: 17, Ecclesiastes 11: 1)

    3. "Now" (2 Corinthians 6: 2)

IV

IF WE WOULD WIN TO CHRIST

We consider first some general requisites to success in winning to Christ, and then we present some requisites which are more personal.

I. GENERAL REQUISITES

1. *A first necessity is to create and maintain an atmosphere for such winning.* That strange, indefinable something which we call atmosphere! In all matters of life and growth we are coming more and more to value its fine power. All life, vegetable, animal, human, yields to this impelling power. Certainly in the realm of evangelism and in all matters of spiritual life and growth it is difficult to estimate the power and meaning of atmosphere. There are happy seasons when it seems easy to speak for Christ, seasons when such effort seems readily to prevail. A blessed revival has recently brought refreshing to the city in which the writer lives. A comment frequently heard is, "It is so easy to speak to lost men." A casual conversation may readily drift into a personal invitation to seek the Lord. It was not so in other days before the revival came. What it is? For want of more accurate designation, we may call it *atmosphere*.

There are communities in which it is fairly impossible to offer Christ in simple and confident fashion. The most zealous evangelistic spirit is quenched and repelled by the iciness which prevails. In other communities it is difficult to withhold the evangelistic note. A worker took part in a great Sunday school occasion. Finding the atmosphere clearly favorable to evangelism, he set aside his prepared message and brought a simple appeal and invitation to accept Christ. Seventeen responded, and all

were shortly afterwards baptized into the fellowship of
the church. It was that fine, intangible something which
we call atmosphere and which every spiritual soul in-
stinctively feels.

Mrs. Lamareaux tells of a woman who was leaving a
home in which she had been a guest for some weeks. "I
do not know what it is," she said to her hostess, "I cannot define it, but there is something about you which has
made me want to be good. I had not been in your home
a week before I felt a strange impulse to seek higher
things. Alone in my room after others had retired, I
got out my long-neglected Bible, knelt down and gave
myself anew to God. I can't tell what it is, but something
about you led me back to God." We know very well
what it was, that fine flavor of life which comes of high
living and earnest praying.

It is not easy to create and maintain such atmosphere.
Not the pastor alone, nor yet the pastor, the superintendent and the teachers, can create such spiritual con-
ditons. All the estates of Israel must join hands and
hearts and prayers for the high task.

2. *We must train the child for this end.* Whether the
child will early yield to Christ and publicly confess him
must depend much on what the child knows and what
the child is as the result of the training and influences
which have marked the earlier years. The delicate, sensitive soul of the child may, by an atmosphere of prayer
and by holy teaching, be given a bias, a distinct bent,
toward Jesus.

We will need to train the child *for* Christ. Because
we hope that the child will some day be Christ's witness
and messenger, we will wish patiently to build into his
life all possible elements of strength and beauty.

We will train the child *toward* Christ. As we have seen,
there is such a thing as preparing for conversion. The
mother dealing with the little child will carefully train
toward Christ; the beginner and primary teacher will
catch up the process and help to carry it forward.

We will train *in* Christ. When we have brought the
child to Christ, our task is only fairly begun. Then we
are to nurture and cultivate the child in all the deep and
precious things of Jesus. There are certain habits which
early fixed on the child make his conversion exceedingly
improbable. The worker who will win the child to Jesus
will guard against these pernicious habits; he will seek
to plant the holy habits of prayer, Bible-reading, church
attendance. He will train the child with a view to his
early conversion.

3. *We must train the teachers to this end.* Whatever
we want in the Sunday school we should train for. If
we desire better teaching, we train for it. If evangelism
is desirable and in a sense pre-eminent, why may we not
train for it?

A church community got this vision of training for soul-
winning. The officers and teachers were drawn together in
a special class to study and train for evangelism. These
workers assembled for a blessed hour each week in an
upper room to pray and search the Scriptures. They used
as a textbook Doctor Torrey's *How to Bring Men to
Christ*. They studied together the various problems
of practical evangelism, how to open the subject of personal religion, how to deal with various difficulties, how to
lead various types of people, and especially how to use
the Word in dealing with the lost.

When these seasons of prayerful preparation had continued for some weeks, a teacher came to the pastor
just before the Sunday evening service, her face lighted
with joy, and said, "Pastor, a year ago my little girl
came home from church desiring to know the Lord. I
was as helpless as if I had been a child myself. I called
you in and you took my crown. I remember well how
easily you led my child to accept and trust the Saviour.
This morning my little boy came home under conviction
for sin. I detected instantly the Spirit's presence; I had
been studying in the soul-winner's class; I knew what
to say and do. I took my child into a room alone,

turned to Isaiah 53: 1-6, and told him the sweet, simple story of Jesus and his atoning death. Then we prayed together, my child and I, and it was my joy to see him give his heart to the Saviour." Within three months after the inauguration of that training class, some forty had, through the efforts of the teachers, yielded to the Saviour. We will train the teachers for personal work in dealing with the lost.

4. *We must teach for this end.* Our teaching, if our hearts are full of this spirit of evangelism, will be flavored by it. There will be the evangelistic note running through all of our instruction. But there is a certain vital and definite content of truth which is especially needful and which the teacher must see that the child shall come to know. This concerns the sinfulness of sin and the holiness of God, the atonement of Jesus wrought out in his sacrificial life and death, the duty of every soul to repent and believe the gospel. The teacher who knows these things by a deep and sweet experience of them and who teaches them to the young, will not find it difficult to win the pupils early to love and trust the Saviour.

5. *We must secure information with a view to winning to Christ.* To secure full and accurate information is a first step toward intelligent effort. Indeed, a failure to seek such information convicts us of indifference and sloth. The jeweler who possesses rare and costly stones has each stone carefully listed, and is able to tell at a moment's notice the history and worth of each of his gems. Can the pastor or teacher afford to be less accurately informed as regards the priceless lives the Father has entrusted to his care?

Some time ago the United States government took a "bird census." In order the better to protect and care for its beautiful feathered creatures, the government sent out a vast army of men and women into all parts of the country to count its birds and to secure needed information concerning their habits. If a great country

is thus careful of its birds, how much more should we
be careful and diligent in securing and keeping accurate
data concerning the imperishable children whom God
has entrusted to us! The mere process of securing such
information will awaken interest, while the information
itself will be a challenge to effort.

A pastor led his forces along these lines with the result that more than fifty pupils were converted in the
regular services in three months. In the workers' council
the pastor laid it on the hearts of the officers and teachers
that the supreme thing in Sunday school work is to win
to Christ. For a season every energy was to be bent
toward this one thing.

As preparatory and preliminary to the work in hand,
full and accurate information was secured in all departments from the Juniors up. For the purpose of securing
accurate information and at the same time giving notice
in all circles of what was proposed, the teachers were
urged to visit the pupils and interview them personally.
As helpful for guidance and training, information was to
be secured in all cases, whether the pupils were church
members or not. Cards were prepared for this purpose.

When these cards had been filled out with the desired
information, they were assorted by departments and set
before the workers' council. Announcement, in the Junior
department, for example, was made somewhat as follows:
"Here in these two sets of cards is complete information
regarding our Junior department. Here are twenty-six
cards for Juniors who are already in the church. Here
are forty-four cards which give information concerning
Juniors who are not saved."

Statement was made in like manner in connection with
each department. Information about as follows was
presented: Forty-four Juniors, thirty-six Intermediates,
nineteen young people and eleven adults were without
Christ, a total of one hundred ten. Here, then, were the
"possibilities" of that school in the matter of soul-
winning. All vagueness was dispelled, all uncertainty

was gone. Duplicate copies of the cards were made
and each teacher was given a full record of the lost
in his class. All went in to work together, by personal
approach, by appeals from the platform, in the Sunday
school and preaching services, by every possible means,
for the salvation of the one hundred ten whose names
were listed. From week to week, in special sessions
of the workers' council, the cards were checked
up and those who were being saved were taken from the
list of the unconverted and added to the list of the saved.
At the end of three months it was found that fifty-five
had been baptized.

In order to secure a definite committal to seek the Lord,
the unconverted were asked to sign the following card:

SEEKING JESUS

Knowing myself to be a sinner in need of a Saviour, I
desire to seek the Lord and become a Christian. I ask the
prayers of the church that I may be saved.

Name ....

Grade (or age) ....

Address ....

For God so loved the world that he gave his only begotten Son, that whosoever believeth in him should not
perish, but have everlasting life (John 3: 16).

In order to keep accurate information and also to
send the announcement to the home, pupils who accepted
Christ were asked to sign in duplicate the following card,
one copy being kept by the pastor, the other being sent
to the parents:

CONFESSION CARD

As a sinner lost and helpless, I take Jesus to be my Saviour from sin. I love him, and trust him as my Saviour and Lord. It is my desire to be baptized in his name and it is my purpose to obey and serve him.

Name ....

Grade (or age) ....

Address ....

As many as received him, to them gave he power to become the sons of God, even to them that believe on his name (John 1: 12).

A well-known evangelist returned to his home after a season of absence. The day before his return a girl in her early teens had died and the family desired the evangelist to conduct the services. He walked down to the home and, in conversation with the father, said, "I ought to know, but I am away from home so much; was Mary a professed Christian?" The father said sadly, "I do not take as much interest in those things as I ought; her mother will know; we will ask her." When the mother came in, she confessed that she did not know, but the *pastor* was faithful and careful in these matters; *he* would know. The pastor was consulted. He did not recall, but the *superintendent* knew the young people well, and was always concerned for their spiritual welfare; he would know. But the superintendent did not know. He felt sure, however, that Mary's *teacher* would know. Alas, the teacher sorrowfully confessed, "I had long intended to speak to Mary about the Saviour. Somehow I neglected to do so, and now she is gone from us." Thus the young life had slipped through the hands of pastor and superintendent, of teacher and parents, and the soul had gone away to meet God without a single earnest effort to bring her to accept Jesus.

The superintendent and pastor surely ought to know every pupil, his spiritual condition, whether he has manifested an interest, whether he has made a confession of Jesus, whether his parents are saved and whether his home influence is spiritually wholesome. Cards suitable for securing this information may be printed at small expense.

II. SOME PERSONAL REQUISITES

1. *There must be a strong conviction of the sinfulness of sin and of the sufficiency of the atoning work of Jesus.* One must know the plan of salvation, not only intellectually, and not alone by an experience of grace, but by a present vivid knowing. The joy of this present knowledge must be real and keen. The Psalmist prayed, "Restore unto me the joy of thy salvation; and uphold me with thy free spirit. *Then* will I teach transgressors thy ways; and sinners shall be converted unto thee" (Psalm 51: 12).

2. *We must have compassion for lost souls.* Jesus in all of his glorious ministry felt such compassion for the lost. His miracles of healing are marked by the desire to reach and save men's souls. Read again, and on your knees, his matchless parables in Luke 15, the Lost Coin, the Lost Sheep, the Lost Son. In the threefold picture rising constantly higher in dignity and pathos, see inside the heart of the Son of man and catch his outlook on human life. That fine, ceaseless concern for the souls of men, that passionate grief for their sins, lends a nameless charm to his life and ministry. This constitutes its deathless power.

This love for the lost is essential in all soul-winning work. There is no substitute for it; not culture, nor Bible knowledge, nor zeal, can take its place. This heart-compassion is part of the price which the Christ paid that he might redeem us. It is the price we must pay if we will share in his glorious redeeming work. What a word is that word of Paul: "I fill up that which is behind of the afflictions of Christ" (Colossians 1: 24). The sufferings of Jesus go out for the lost, but they do not quite reach the lost until we "fill up that which is lacking" by standing with our crushed hearts between the suffering Saviour and the lost soul.

3. *There must be a working knowledge of the Bible.* This does not mean that one who would win souls must needs be a finished Bible scholar. It does mean that he should know how to use the Bible to show the fact and reality of sin, the sufficiency of the saving work of our Lord, and the duty of immediate acceptance of the offer of salvation. This content of Bible knowledge is set forth in a later discussion.

4. *We must live for this end.* Surely this is a high purpose for which any teacher will do well to live! A teacher was urged to attend a place of amusement concerning which there was some question. She declined, saying, "I am living for the salvation of my pupils. I would almost rather see them in their graves than to see them caught and swept by tides of gayety and godlessness." A few weeks later a revival was on, and that teacher had the joy of seeing twelve beautiful girls give themselves to the Saviour. She had lived to this end.

A Christian woman was soon to be married to a young man of choice family but of worldly habits. A few weeks before the wedding the young man said to some of his dissolute companions, "I know what you fellows think; you think that I will not be married to that woman six months before I will be as pious as a deacon and be going to Sunday school and church. You just wait and see. Before I have been married to that woman six months she will be going with me to dances and card parties and in the ways of the world." A few months after the wedding, the young couple moved into their own little cottage home. In the evening of the first day,

they sat alone together. The young woman brought out
her Bible and said: "John, I know that you don't take
much stock in these things, but I want our new home to be
a religious home. My father's house was a house of
prayer; I cannot recall the time when we did not have
our altar of worship. I want our home to be a house of
prayer." They sat together a few minutes without further
word; he was considering the simple plea of his young
wife and was secretly admiring her courage. "And now,"
she said, "I know that you do not much believe in these
things, but if you do not mind, I want to read some verses
from this Book." She read the verses, but her husband,
yielding to a rebellious spirit, refused to listen and continued to read the afternoon paper. Firmly resolved to
win out that first night in the new home, the young
woman said: "I know how you feel about these things,
but our home *must* be a place of prayer. I do not know
whether I can do such a thing or not because I never
tried to pray before any one else, but if you don't mind,
I am going to try to pray." Some days later the young
man was telling his companions of this experience: "I
swore I would not have anything to do with religion; I
was determined that I would not get on my knees. But,
fellows, before I knew it I was down first on one knee;
then on both knees; then I put my face on the very floor;
as she prayed she put one hand on my head and with
the other she seemed to reach up toward the throne of
God. And—well—there is no human being who could
touch that woman's life without being made better." Back
of that crucial hour and lending power to the appeal was
the life which that woman had lived.

THINK ON THESE THINGS:

What is meant by "an atmosphere for winning"?
"We must train the child to this end." Discuss this statement.
What of training teachers for soul-winning?
How may we secure information with a view to winning to Christ?

Why the necessity of "compassion for lost souls"?
What working knowledge of the Bible is needed?
Discuss the suggestion that "we must live for this end."

CHAPTER OUTLINE

If We Would Win to Christ

I. General Requisites
  1. Create a favorable atmosphere
  2. Train the child
  3. Train the teachers
  4. Teach for this end
  5. Secure information

II. Some Personal Requisites
  1. Clear conviction of plan of salvation
  2. Compassion for lost souls
  3. Working knowledge of the Bible
  4. We must live for this end

V

DEALING WITH THE INDIVIDUAL

We come now to the crux of the whole matter. In all efforts to win to Christ, it is personality and the personal touch that count for most. A wise, tactful, personal appeal, backed by holy living, will almost certainly prevail.

I. Why Deal with the Individual?

The reasons are many and they are very weighty.

1. *This was the method of Jesus.* In the first chapter of John's gospel, we have some vivid pictures showing how the new gospel era was ushered in, and illustrating for all time the effective method of winning the lost.

John the Baptist led two of his disciples to follow Jesus —Andrew and probably John.

Andrew findeth his brother Simon and *brought* him to Jesus.

Jesus *findeth* Philip and said unto him, "Follow me."

Philip *findeth* Nathanael and said, "Come and see."

2. *The issues at stake demand it.* A woman dressed in silks and satins was walking along a street in Paris, when she dropped from her finger into the filth and slime of the gutter a valuable jewel. She stopped instantly. Under her arm she bore an elegant sunshade with a crooked handle. Using the crook, she searched the gutter for her jewel. It was not to be found that way. Then, to the astonishment of the crowd, she stripped her glove from her dainty white hand, rolled up above her elbow her sleeve of costly lace, and, with delicate pink fingers bared, she searched the gutter and found her jewel. Is not this our task, with eager zeal to search even the very gutters for the gems of human life?

3. *This method is most effectual.* The author has occasionally, in conducting revival services, raised the question before audiences as to how many were won to Christ
by sermons or general appeals, and how many came to
Christ as the result of a direct personal effort and appeal
on the part of some faithful believer. The response has
been uniformly the same, a majority always declaring
that they had sought and found the Lord because of
the effort of some individual.

(1) It is the most effectual for the preacher. An
evangelistic pastor in Cincinnati some time ago laid his
hand on the arm of a fine young man as he was leaving
the church, looked him in the eye, and asked him if he
was a Christian. The young man, evidently welcoming
the question, replied, "No sir, I have heard you preach
every Sunday for seven years, but I am not a Christian." The two walked together into the pastor's study
and within five minutes the young man had made the
great surrender and declared his faith in Jesus Christ.
Seven years of brilliant preaching had failed; five minutes alone together and the soul was won. The minister
can instruct and impress from the pulpit, but in order to
win he must come into close "grips" with the lost.

(2) It is likewise effectual for the teacher. A choice
boy presented himself for church membership one Sunday
morning.

"Harry," said the pastor, "how does it happen that
you are here? There is no revival on, and others are
not seeking the Lord; tell us how it is that you come confessing Christ."

Harry studied for a moment and then said, "It is like
this: last Sunday morning my teacher said, 'Wouldn't you
like to walk with me in the park this afternoon? I
have something very important I want to talk with you
about.' Now, we boys are always glad to be with our
teacher, so I said, 'Sure, you may count on me.' At four
o'clock my teacher and I were walking together in the
park. We sat down on a rustic seat, and my teacher said,

'Harry, I want you for the Lord Jesus. I have long prayed for this, and I asked you to come out here with me alone that we might settle this great question.' Out there in the park I gave my heart to the Lord, and now I want to be baptized and live among his people."

What is true of the preacher and of the teacher is equally true of every other worker; if we will win men we must deal with them personally; nothing can take the place of the personal touch.

(3) Church officers have found that the individual approach will prevail. Johnston Myers tells how a faithful minister assembled his official board and opened his heart to them, telling them of his conviction that the deepest need in the church which they served was personal effort and individual approach to the lost. He told them of his deep concern because souls were not being saved. And he declared with much earnestness his conviction that the failure of the church was probably due to their failure in that they were not going personally to the lost to warn them of their peril. He asked how many had ever won a soul to the Saviour. Only two out of the fifteen present had reason to believe that they had ever been thus used.

As the pastor pressed this duty on their consciences, the men were aroused and tears attested their deep conviction. One of the men, a banker, had four sons grown to manhood who had never confessed Christ. His heart smote him for his neglect. He left the room in silence. He hurried to his home resolved to make amends for his neglect. Before the morning's dawn, he had talked and prayed separately with each of those four sons and had besought them to seek the Lord. The next Sunday those four sons presented themselves for membership in the church. The next morning when this banker went into his office, the first man who came in to see him was a trusted employee who was not a Christian. Closing the door the banker said to the young man, "I have something to talk to you about. I am glad we are alone. Do you know that I have been a Christian ever since we have known each other?"

The man stood dazed before him, but replied, "Yes."

"Do you know that I am now an elder in the Presbyterian Church?"

Still more surprised, he replied, "Yes."

"Haven't you thought it strange that I never spoke to you about your relation to Christ?"

"Yes, sir," said the man, "and I have been in your office a hundred times and not only wondered why you didn't say it, but waited for you to do so."

Doctor Myers declares that in that business office that morning another soul was added to Jesus, and thus one church officer learned the joy and experienced the power of a personal dealing with lost men.

(4) Parents likewise must depend on the face-to-face individual appeal. Some one tells of a boy who came to confess Christ. When the pastor asked him what brought him to Jesus, the rather startling reply was, "A cigarette." Then the boy hastened to explain: "I smoked my first cigarette. I did so in secret, but my father somehow discovered my sin. I thought he would be angry, and expected him to punish me. Instead, my father sorrowfully talked to me of his pain for my folly, and then told me of his grief for my sins in general. He told me how much he wanted to see me come to Christ. And, sir, I knelt down alone with my father and right there I gave myself to the Lord."

II. How Shall We Deal with the Individual?

1. *Win respect* and *affection.* It is, of course, essential first of all that we who would win to Christ shall command the unqualified respect of those whom we would win. Young people especially are exacting in their demands. Their standards are somewhat inflexible and their demands are rigid. Later they will learn to make allowance and will know more of the temptations and battles of life. At present they have their ideals, and

woe to their elders if they fall short or in any wise disappoint their expectations! It is possible in one single hour of laxity or swerving to shatter the confidence of the adolescent boy or girl.

It is scarcely less important to win love. It is one thing to command respect; it is a higher thing to draw out love. A teacher stood alone with her pupil in the quiet of the evening: "Louise, do you love me?" For response the girl pressed the teacher's hand and gave her an impulsive kiss. "But, Louise, if you love me, I want you to love my Saviour." How many children and older people have come to love Jesus because they had learned to love some one whose life is devoted to him!

2. *Seize the opportune time.* This is always a matter of prime consequence in winning the lost. There are critical moments when the Spirit seems to set ajar all doors of approach to the soul—moments when the gentlest whisper will penetrate to the deep recesses of the heart. Such times may come at the most unexpected seasons. We should watch for them as the watchman watches for the morning. It may be that under the teaching of a lesson or under a sermon the Spirit will begin his work and will call for our co-operation to carry that work to completion in salvation. It may be that some sorrow or disappointment will bring the opportune time. Such time will most likely come all unexpectedly and there may be nothing more than a sigh, a question, a yearning in the voice to serve notice that the way is open for the word touching the Saviour.

"I remember very well," wrote a young man, "the morning I packed up my things to go and fill a situation in the city, how my mother prayed for me and said, as she thought of the temptations I should be subject to, 'Oh, William, how I wish you were a Christian!' I wished so, too. She hoped all would be right. When that day I went into the garden to say goodbye to father and he saw me coming, he turned his head to hide the tears, and he reached out his calloused hand, calloused for me, and bade me seek the Saviour. I promised him I would, and I did." That father and mother, after years of waiting, spoke at an opportune time, and their son was converted.

3. *Find out and remove barriers.* Much of our effort in soul-winning is ineffective because we fail at this point. We may urge a person to believe and trust Christ, when we might do better to seek out the secret indulgence, the unseen influence, which stands between the soul and Christ, and urge the confession and removal of the sin which constitutes the unsurmountable barrier.

A young man was under conviction for sin, and in distress and with evident sincerity was seeking the Lord. A Christian worker gave the usual instruction, presented again and again the way of life, but was disappointed in being unable to lead the seeking one to the Saviour. The two knelt to pray together and the worker asked the seeker to offer the prayer, "Our Father which art in heaven," and so forth. He proceeded to the petition, "Forgive us our debts as we forgive our debtors." Here the voice ceased and the suppliant refused to proceed. Suddenly it dawned upon the worker that an unforgiving spirit stood in the way. In tender but faithful words it was made clear that this sin must be confessed and forsaken. At last, in slow, measured tones, the words were uttered, "Forgive us our debts as we forgive our debtors." Immediately the light dawned, and there was a sense of peace and acceptance with God.

A determination to hold to some sinful amusement, an obstinate refusal to do something which the Christian life may seem to require, may keep the soul from the kingdom of God. Be faithful; urge complete surrender and final submission.

4. *Seek proficiency in conducting a religious conversation.*

(1) Study how to open a conversation. Nicodemus opened the great subject, having taken the initiative in seeking Jesus. Not so the woman of Samaria. Her mind

was bent upon material things. In an emergency situation she had come in the heat of the noon hour to secure water for her household. It was necessary for Jesus to open the conversation and lift the mind of the woman up to spiritual planes.

Just here often is the soul-winner's most difficult problem. How shall he get started? With what words is he to turn the conversation from earthly to heavenly things? Jesus began by asking a favor. Tactful beyond words he was. "Woman, give me a drink." He asked a favor; at the same time, he bestowed a favor. He would accept a kindness at the hands of this strange woman. Instantly the conversation was opened and quickly Jesus led on to the word which he desired to speak.

Once a start is made and the subject is broached, it is usually easy to make headway. But how shall we get started?

If the person whom we would approach has attended Sunday school or has been in a preaching service, it may be simple enough to begin by saying:

"I have seen you in some of our worship services; I hope you are a Christian"; or, we may say, "I should be glad if I might be of service to you in helping you to find the Lord."

If we do not know the person very well, we may open a conversation by saying:

"Perhaps I ought to know; I hope that you will not think me impertinent, if I ask, Are you a Christian?"

Possibly we may wish to introduce the subject of a personal acceptance of Christ by a simple word of testimony somewhat as follows:

"I have much comfort in Jesus as my Lord and Saviour. I have leaned on his strength and he has never failed me. I wonder if you would let me talk to you about him."

A method often pursued by seekers after the lost is to present a brief leaflet with a striking title and ask the person to read it. When the leaflet has been read it will

be natural to fall into a discussion of the question which
it raises.

A method of approach which has much to commend
it is to come straight to the great question by saying:

"My friend, I want the privilege of talking with you
about my Saviour. I wish you knew him. You would
like to be a Christian, wouldn't you?"

Skill in winning to Christ comes with intelligent and
persistent practice. Those who have won the greatest
proficiency have often declared that in the beginning
they were painfully diffident. Dr. R. A. Torrey did much
by his example and his teachings to set forward personal
evangelism. Confessedly he was wise and eminently
successful in his efforts to introduce men to Christ. Those
who think of him as a master in the art of winning men
may be surprised to read this statement of his initial
effort:

I do not think that any one could begin more awkwardly in this work than I did with the first person
whom I led to Christ. I felt that God wanted me to
speak to this young man, and I called on him for that
purpose, but when I met him I had not the slightest
idea what to say. I talked on and on waiting for an
opportunity and at last I blundered out awkwardly
what I had come for. God blessed the awkward, but
honest effort, and the young man was saved.

Most of us must begin awkwardly, but as Doctor Torrey well says, we would better begin awkwardly than
not begin at all. The only way to learn to do personal
work is by doing it. Tact comes by experience and practice.

(2) When a conversation is once opened, hold the person to the main question and press for a decision if there
seems to be real concern. Generally, lost people will seek
to divert conversation into less pertinent and less personal lines. Nicodemus met the insistence of Jesus that
he must be born again with a diverting and almost
querulous question about the mystery and the possibility

of being born again. Jesus held steadily to his insistence
and refused to be diverted.

Even more skilfully the Samaritan woman sought to
evade the probe which Jesus was thrusting into her secret
life by raising a much-discussed question as to where men
ought to worship God. But Jesus told her plainly that
the duty to worship God was more vital than the question as to where he was to be worshiped. He held steadily
on his course until he had aroused the woman's conscience
and led her to see and accept himself as Saviour.

Skill, of course, will come with experience and practice.
But a first necessity which every soul-winner must encounter is to hold to the main question and prevent di-
gression into questions which may not be profitable.

(3) In conducting a conversation the seeker will wish
to guard against interruptions. Imagine, if you can, how
serious it would have been if some one had broken in on
Jesus in the midst of that eager conversation with Nicodemus. Or, consider what it might have meant if the
disciples had returned while Jesus was leading the
Samaritan woman step by step to realize her own sinfulness and to accept him as her Saviour. Interruptions
cannot always be avoided and when they come we are
to be patient and courteous and make the best of any
trying situation. But the wise winner of souls will, in
so far as may be practicable, safeguard against possible
intrusions or disturbances.

5. *Pray much.* Whoever will win souls must be much
in prayer. God has appointed certain means, such as
his Word and preaching and teaching, for bringing to
salvation. But these are not sufficient apart from the
Holy Spirit. No sinner ever came under conviction of
sin save by the power of the Spirit. No sinner ever
apprehended the Atonement of Jesus and appropriated
its provisions, save through the blessed Spirit. Whatever gifts we possess, whatever influences we bring to
bear, we must rely first and last on the divine Spirit to
do his mighty work in the heart.

The Holy Spirit is given in answer to prayer. The first Pentecost came at the end of ten days of ceaseless prayer. "If ye then, being evil, know how to give good gifts unto your children, how much more shall your heavenly Father give the Holy Spirit to them that ask him" (Luke 11: 13). It is needful that we shall importune the lost to turn to God, but we may not forget nor neglect to importune God to be gracious to the lost.

Successful soul-winners, without exception, have been faithful and urgent in prayer. They rely on God for guidance as to the persons whom they shall approach, and as to the time and method of such approach. They wait on God for power—that strange, indefinable, irresistible power which comes through the anointing of the Spirit. When their efforts seem to fail and hearts are as steel, they turn confidently to God and wait for help. They breathe the very breath of prayer and live in its holy atmosphere.

As superintendent of the Bushwick Avenue Methodist Sunday School in Brooklyn, Mr. Frank L. Brown saw 6,500 members of his school confess Christ and seek church membership. He tells of one of his teachers who brought three successive classes to Christ. As the last girl in her last class confessed Christ, Mr. Brown declared that her face was radiant. He asked her,

"Kate, how did you do it?"

"Mr. Brown," she said, "I remember every one of my girls every day by name in prayer."

6. *Press for a decision.* Much of our effort to win the lost fails because we do not dare to close in and strike for a verdict. We bear witness in timid fashion and hasten to leave the lost soul in its indecision. Joshua's memorable word, "Choose you *this* day whom ye will serve," should be our urgent plea. Are we not commissioned to *compel* them to come in? Such urgency and insistence is proper from every viewpoint. The peril to which the lost soul is exposed, the yearning love of the divine heart, the promise of immediate pardon to

those who yield, these and other high and worthy considerations demand that we shall patiently and persistently press for a decision.

THINK ON THESE THINGS:

Why is evangelism necessarily personal?

Give some reasons why we should deal with the individual.

Cite instances to show that personal evangelism was the method used by Jesus in winning men.

Offer suggestions for dealing with the individual.

Suggest incidents coming under your own observation which attest the power of the personal approach.

Offer in detail some suggestions as to how a conversation with lost people may be opened.

What counsel would you offer as to the conduct of a conversation with an unsaved person?

Is it proper to draw the inference from our insistence upon personal evangelism that preaching or mass evangelism is not effective? Why?

CHAPTER OUTLINE

I. Why Deal with the Individual?
  1. This was the method of Jesus
  2. The issues at stake demand it
  3. The method is most effectual
    (1) For the preacher
    (2) For the teacher
    (3) For the church officers
    (4) For parents

II. How Shall We Deal with the Individual?
  1. Win respect and affection
  2. Seize the opportune time
  3. Find out and remove barriers
  4. Seek efficiency in conducting a religious conversation
  5. Pray much
  6. Press for a decision

VI

WINNING THROUGH THE SUNDAY SCHOOL

We have already intimated that a chief agency at present depended on in evangelistic effort is the Sunday school. This fact is now so generally recognized that it does not call for discussion. In this chapter we seek to show how soul-winning efforts may be conducted through the Sunday school.

I. A CONTACT MEDIUM

A first problem in winning to Christ is to find contacts on which winning efforts may be based. In other days the mere announcement of a "revival meeting" was usually sufficient to draw people in considerable, and often very great, numbers. It was not difficult to get access to the popular masses, and even lost people could be induced in goodly numbers to hear the appeals of the gospel.

This is now very largely changed. A first difficulty which faces us in any plan to win to Christ is to get a hearing, to secure contacts of some kind. Lost people do not in any considerable numbers attend preaching services. Certainly they do not any more flock to our special revival meetings. The same may with equal emphasis be said of people who have moved their residence without moving their church membership. A visiting evangelist preached at the eleven o'clock hour in a certain city. In the afternoon a considerable gathering of church workers assembled for prayer and conference. The question was raised in this group as to how many lost people or unaffiliated believers were in the audience at the morning hour. It developed that no Christian worker could recall the presence at the morning service of any lost or unaffiliated people. This was doubtless somewhat exceptional but if the reader would make the test in his own Sunday morning audience he might be surprised at the results.

There are, to be sure, conditions and sections in which these statements will not hold, but in general they will be recognized as sufficiently accurate. How, then, are the necessary contacts for the initial efforts in winning to be secured?

The sure medium, a method now widely used and amply tested, is the Sunday school. It is hardly too much to say that the Sunday school under present-day conditions offers the one sure and dependable medium for establishing contacts looking toward winning to Christ. We do not seem able to draw the lost and the backslidden in any considerable numbers directly to our preaching services; we do not seem any longer to succeed in attracting them to our revival meetings. But we can and we do draw them into our Sunday schools.

Churches and church workers which stand for a regenerated membership cannot feel at liberty to urge people indiscriminately to unite with the church. They do not wish to see people unite with the church until they have sought and found Christ as a personal Saviour. There can be no such hesitancy in urging people to join the Sunday school. This school of the church sets wide open its doors to saints and sinners, to happy believers, and wandering backsliders. This method of establishing contact through the Sunday school is scientific and sure. It has been amply demonstrated in churches large and small; it has been tested in churches located in city, town, and country.

II. A WINNING MEDIUM

The Sunday school by its very genius lends itself to the establishment of contacts with spiritually needy people. It offers a happy medium for winning the lost to Christ. Beginning with the teacher the circle of winners widens through the department superintendent and the general superintendent out to the pastor. Let us look at this group of winners.

1. *There is the teacher.* We name the teacher first because the teacher is first. He is first in responsibility, first in opportunity, and first in potential influence. Classes are generally small. Lost pupils are placed in the same classes with saved pupils. Besides the Sunday contacts, there are the week-day social and recreational contacts. Could there be a better arrangement for winning to Christ?

2. *Then comes next in line the department superintendent.* Back of the teacher, aiding, inspiring, and challenging him in his winning efforts is the department superintendent. This superintendent as well as the teachers should have the names of the lost in each class and he should constantly support the teachers and co-operate with them in their efforts to win the lost to Christ. Such a list of the lost may be made up from the Six Point Record System, though it will probably be necessary to correct and verify any records used as a source of information so that absolute accuracy in names and addresses may be assured. From the Junior department up through the Adult department, the department superintendent may wish to check up in the weekly teachers' meeting or in the monthly workers' council to see what progress is being made and to give definite encouragement to the teachers in their winning efforts.

3. *Back of the teacher and the department superintendent comes the general superintendent.* He will seek to challenge the department superintendent and the teachers to constant and diligent efforts to win the lost to Christ and the unaffiliated to unite with the church. He may also wish to keep on file by departments and classes the names of the lost and he may wish to check up on this list with his associates from time to time.

4. *Back of all these, of course, is the pastor.* He will likewise wish to keep lists of the unsaved by depart-

ments and classes and he will seek to send down through the whole organization appeals and messages and challenges which will keep alive everywhere the winning spirit.

It is not difficult to see how potentially at least this is a most effective mechanism for reaching the lost. For every lost person four people are directly responsible. First and nearest to him with most direct responsibility is the teacher. Back of the teacher, cheering him and seconding his efforts or responding to his appeal for help, is the department superintendent. Back of the teacher and the department superintendent stands the general superintendent. This general officer seconds the winning efforts of his associates and holds himself ready to respond as they may need help. Back of the three stands the pastor who will second the efforts of all the others and be the general inspirer in all that they undertake to do. This ought to be an undefeatable combination.

Is it possible that these four people working and praying together for a whole year will be unable to win a lost boy or girl to Christ? Suppose that they should fail in a given year. When a new year opens there is a new teacher for that lost boy or girl. The new teacher is again backed by the department superintendent, the general superintendent, and the pastor. Suppose this group should fail. When each new year opens there is a new formation with a new teacher and a fresh opportunity to win.

Besides these four who should stand solidly for the winning of each lost person in the Sunday school, we may name, and should name, the parents. Whether they are themselves saved or not, the father and mother will in all probability stand on our side as we seek to win their children to Christ. There is that in the heart of a father which, when we probe down deep enough, longs to see his children know and serve God. There is likewise that in the heart of motherhood which causes the mother to desire her children to be right with God. It seems to be an instinct divinely implanted in the parental heart. When the four people indicated above move toward seeking the lost in any home they may with assurance count at least on the passive sympathy of the father and mother.

This outline of suggestion was presented to a group in which was a salesman of wide experience whose chief business it is to train salesmen and to promote salesmanship. This man listened intently and when the opportunity offered he spoke somewhat as follows: "This plan for seeking the lost is without flaw. Properly worked it is bound to win. From the time a child enters the Junior department to the time he comes to maturity there will be twenty teachers seeking his salvation, each backed by an interested group of sympathetic workers. Even after that time on through the years the organized classes will be in line seeking to win him. That combination and arrangement cannot be excelled anywhere in all the world."

III. Each of the Four Workers Mentioned Above Must Stand in Line and Make His Contribution

1. *The teacher stands closest to the lost and has of course a prime responsibility.* A pastor evangelist was assisting a brother pastor in a special revival effort. These men had secured full lists of the possibilities and had planned to visit the lost in their classes. Miss Mary ———— was a teacher of Juniors with several lost girls in her class. She was a choice young woman possessed of rare charms.

"Miss Mary," said the pastor, "here is a list of lost girls in your class. Will you take these names and visit these girls in the effort to win them to the Saviour?"

"I am sorry, but I cannot go."

The pastor felt that he could not take such an answer as final. If this gracious and gifted woman should decline to go, her refusal would have a widely discouraging influence. He paused and prayed, as he waited expectantly.

"Pastor," said the young woman, "I can't go and ask those girls to accept Christ. I have no reason to think that I have myself been saved. I never had in my own heart such an experience as I have many times heard you describe. Now you will understand why I cannot go."

There was a tense moment. Many heads were bowed as silent prayers ascended to the Father.

"Miss Mary," said the pastor, "will you come with me into the study for a few minutes?"

As the young woman arose to follow the pastor, two devout women went with them. The visiting minister went on with the assignments until presently the pastor and the three women came out of the study. Miss Mary's face was shining with a new light and her friends perceived that a great change had come over her.

When the company was seated, the pastor said very quietly, "Miss Mary, you will tell your own story."

Many hearts were beating fast and all leaned forward in expectancy as the young woman rose to her feet.

"In yonder room," she began, "with these friends, I confessed my sins and begged God for mercy and pardon. The Saviour heard my cry and saved me." Then turning to the pastor, she said, "Give me the names of those girls. I can go now. I have something to tell them."

The next Sunday morning Miss Mary led nine of her girls down the aisle to confession and church membership.

2. *The department superintendent and the general superintendent stand next in line.* If their hands are off, and they offer no challenge or inspiration, all soul-winning efforts will drag heavily. What shall we do, if these trusted leaders feel no compassion for the lost, show no concern, no care for the lost? Then are we undone, indeed.

3. *Next in line is the pastor.* If his hand is off, and if he does not challenge and guide, sad indeed and all but hopeless must be the situation! The pastor's highest

duty and most difficult task is to keep the fires of soul-winning zeal burning always on the altar of his own heart.

Bishop Adna Wright Leonard of the Methodist Episcopal Church tells in a recent book* how a popular and apparently successful pastor was transformed in his spiritual life. The pastor had invited an evangelist to hold a meeting with him. As the meeting drew to a close the two men talked together in the closest intimacy and in fullest confidence. With pardonable pride the pastor told his visitor that he had been seven years in that pastorate and that he loved the people and had reason to believe that the people loved him.

The evangelist said: "Many of your people have talked to me about you. They love you. They admire your social qualities and they also say that you are a good mixer. But, shall I tell you what else they say?"

The pastor replied, "By all means."

"They say," replied the visiting clergyman, "that you are not giving them a spiritual leadership."

In relating the incident, the pastor said: "When he told me that, I was cut to the quick; but I went home, examined my life and ministry and came to the conclusion that my people were right in their criticism."

The next day was Sunday; the special meetings were closing. In the last service and near the close of the service, the evangelist made earnest plea for a new and deeper consecration. He asked the pastor to lead in prayer. The pastor stepped out to the platform and told of the conversation he had had the day before with the visiting preacher. He added: "Your criticism of me is correct. I have not given you the spiritual leadership you ought to have had. I am truly sorry for the great lack in my ministry. But I have also asked God to forgive me and I have pledged him that from this on my ministry shall be a spiritual ministry and that I will make Christ and his kingdom first. All of you who will follow

*Ancient Fires on Modern Altars. The Abingdon Press.

me as I try to lead out in a truly spiritual ministry, come forward and give me your hand and join me in prayer."

Bishop Leonard declares that upwards of four hundred came forward and grasped the hand of the pastor pledging him that they would live lives of renewed prayer and consecration. From that time, Bishop Leonard tells us, the people of the church witnessed a complete transformation in the life of their pastor. Increased numbers waited on his ministry and with power he appealed to men to forsake sin and trust the Saviour.

Bishop Leonard who relates the above story filled three pastorates before he was chosen to be a bishop. In his first pastorate he resolved to speak to at least one lost person each day about the great question of salvation. He was so blessed in this service and saw such abundant fruits that when he was transferred to another pastorate he resolved to enlarge his winning efforts. He determined to make it a rule to talk each day to at least two lost people. Again, he found such joy in the personal witnessing and saw such manifest results that when he went to a third pastorate he set his heart on dealing personally with at least three lost people each day. The bishop has issued the book to which we have referred, in which he relates some of the happy experiences which he had in this effort to win by personal contact.

The author told in the presence of a company of ministers the above story of pastoral effort in soul-winning. At the close of the hour a pastor drew him aside and said, "Would you let me tell you about my method in seeking the lost?" He drew from his pocket a long list of names and told me that the list represented his "prospects." There were the names of eighty-two Juniors. Then came in the list the names of nearly forty Intermediates. Then followed a great number of Young People and a long list of Adults. The pastor continued:

Every Monday morning I go into my study and pray especially for my Junior boys and girls. I expect that my people will share with me in this ministry of intercession. After the noon hour I go out to visit in the homes where there are unsaved Juniors. On Tuesday I repeat this for the Intermediates. I have a long list of unsaved Young People and I give Wednesday and Thursday to them. Friday morning I engage in prayer for the lost in our Adult department, and Friday afternoon I visit these lost people. In our men's classes we have fifty-two lost men.

Pastors who thus visit and win will generally find it comparatively easy to induce their officers and teachers to visit and win.

IV. What We May Expect of the Departments

We departmentize our schools for the purposes of management and instruction. Gradually we are coming to offer departmental programs for social life. More and more we will seek to do our winning work by departments, offering in each department just the teaching and the appeal needed by the pupils of that department.

1. *What may we expect of the Cradle Roll workers?*

These friends have the children during the first three years of life. Have these workers with little children no part in winning to Christ? We are coming to realize that no period of similar length in all of life is more meaningful in the development of the spiritual life. As Mrs. Lamoreaux has well said, "Born into a social order of which he is an integral part and to which he may make a contribution through his own unique personality, with infinite capacities and latent abilities waiting only the right touch to awaken him, this period of modifiability is the priceless possession of the educator." In these susceptible years the little child is gaining his first impressions not only of the world around him but of God and Jesus and heaven. The concrete teaching of these years may fade from the mind, but the impressions and influences will linger while life lasts.

Mrs. Lamoreaux*, who writes so understandingly of the early childhood period, tells of a young mother who said: "I wish my child might always keep the sensitiveness and the reverence for Jesus Christ which she has now; he seems to be so wonderful to her that she cannot speak his name lightly." The home in which the child was growing up was marked by a refined culture and a deep and sincere devotion to Jesus Christ. "As a wee baby," Mrs. Lamoreaux continues, "before she could comprehend its meaning, her mother would hold her before the Madonna pictures on the wall and in a gentle, low voice would tell her it was the baby Jesus and let her look in silence. She used the same tone in telling her the stories of the Christ child when she was old enough to grasp them, and in the evening prayer at her bedside. It was not artificial, it was the natural expression of the mother's own love and adoration. The baby eyes grew accustomed to the Bible in the hands of the father each morning at the breakfast-table, and she felt the hush of the moment as heads were bowed in prayer. The Heavenly Father was a familiar friend, and the conduct of all was considered in the light of his wishes. From birth, this favored child has breathed in this spiritual atmosphere, and her attitude and love is the result. She can never lose it out of her inner life nor her conduct." In so far as our Cradle Roll workers may help to produce atmospheres like this they may be deciding factors in the glorious work of winning to Christ.

There is of course an indirect ministry of winning which these workers with babies may render. While in the pastorate, the author had the pleasure of welcoming into church membership a young business man and his wife. On the Monday following he was with the man in his office, and ventured to ask him about the influences which brought him to a decision. "It was very simple," the man replied; "some of your workers came over to

---

*The Pupils in the Church School, Mrs. Antoinette A. Lamoreaux. The Judson Press.

my house and asked for the name of our baby for something which they called a Cradle Roll. My wife had never heard of such a thing, but she was greatly pleased with the interest shown in the baby and with the promise of the women that they would pray for the baby each day. I went home one day and my wife met me with tears on her cheeks, saying that the Cradle Roll women had been there and had led her to accept the Saviour. She took my hand and led me into the room where the baby lay asleep, and said to me, 'For the baby's sake and for my sake, I want you to give yourself to the Lord.' I knelt down with my wife beside the sleeping babe and surrendered my heart to God." Both the Cradle Roll and the Extension departments will offer to watchful workers many opportunities to lead souls into the light.

2. *What may we expect of workers with Beginners and Primaries?*

In these golden years from four to eight the child is making ever-widening excursions into the world of knowledge and into the realms of life. In no other five years is life so largely formed and the foundation of character so largely laid. These children ought to be taught to love and revere and obey their Heavenly Father just as they are taught to love and revere and obey their earthly father. The question as to whether Juniors and Intermediates will accept Christ and confess him in baptism will in large measure be determined by the impressions made and the instructions given while they are Beginners and Primaries.

A company of rescue mission workers conducted a religious service at the midnight hour on one of the streets of the downtown section of Atlanta. A sinful woman sat in a window far above the street. She heard hymns which had a wonderfully familiar sound. She listened to messages which stirred sacred memories long buried deep in her heart. When the songs had died away and the pleading words of the Christian workers had vanished, the woman felt a strange tugging at her heart and was

conscious of an unutterable longing for a better life.
Long years before the woman as a little child had lived
in a Christian home and had attended a neighborhood
Sunday school. Her teacher had given her a Bible and
had left in her child heart the appeal of the Lord Jesus.
When the mission workers had gone she sought in her
trunk for that neglected Bible and went down on her
knees to find the Saviour of whom her teacher had told
her in the long-past days.

Now, let us ask, Who won that woman to the Lord
Jesus? Did that company of mission workers win her?
Or was she won by that other company of Sunday school
workers who left with her a Bible and some knowledge
of the love and atoning death of Jesus?

3. *What may we expect of Junior workers?*

The Junior years will be found to be the great harvest
season so far as public confession and baptism are concerned. A certain pastor was accustomed to go at fre-
quent intervals into the Junior department. He would
present the claims of Jesus and ask the saved boys and
girls to come and stand together about him. Then he
would propose that those who desired to seek the Lord
should come also and stand with them while a prayer
was offered. After the prayer and while all sang softly,
the pastor would invite and urge acceptance and public
confession of the Saviour. At certain seasons this pastor
was accustomed to indicate to the teachers that he would
be in his study during the Sunday school hour and would
be pleased to receive for prayer and brief conference any
pupils who might be induced to come to him. Thus he
kept the matter of personal faith pressed upon the growing youths and there can be little wonder that few pupils
in that school ever passed out of the Junior department
unsaved.

We cannot too earnestly insist that boys and girls
should be won to Christ before they leave the Junior department. It has been well said that the time to help
the difficult teen-age best is before the teen-age is reached.

The years preceding the trying turbulent years of early adolescence may be used to develop strength, to form character, and to fortify against the inevitable testings which are to come. By all means, bring the boys and girls to Christ and get them anchored in the church before they leave the Junior department.

4. *What may we expect of Intermediate workers?*

As the years advance the task of the winner becomes more difficult and more complex. It is not difficult to lead the Primary pupil to a deepening reverence for Jesus as Friend and Helper. It is usually a simple task to lead the Junior to accept Christ as Saviour and to confess his Lord in baptism. But the winning of Intermediates is not so simple. The winning efforts of Intermediate leaders may well run along two kindred lines:

(1) They are to win the lost. If the Junior workers have been efficient winners, the number of the unsaved among the Intermediates will not be large. Whether the number be large or small, the unsaved are to be carefully listed, and persistent personal effort is to be made to reach and win the last one.

(2) They are to enrich in Christian character and enlist in Christian service. These pupils in the early years of their fellowship with Jesus and of their membership in his church need above other things the enriching and hallowing influence of Christian teachers. Never again will they so much need the strength and comfort of loving and loyal personalities.

5. *What may we expect of workers with Young People and Adults?*

With the further advance of the years, the winning task becomes at once more urgent and more difficult. The proportion of the unsaved among the more mature pupils will almost certainly decrease. The difficulty of winning to Christ will likewise increase. And yet, tactful effort, persistently made, will bear abundant fruit among men and women who, though they are not personally believers, are yet willing to attend Sunday school for the study of God's Word. Dependable working lists of the unsaved and the unchurched should be kept, and systematic, continuous efforts should be made with regular reports of achievements to the class cabinet.

The Extension department also offers, of course, contacts which may be utilized for winning the lost. Indeed, this should be a major element in the work of this vastly vital ministry.

V. How May the Sunday School Contribute to Special Revival Efforts?

The Sunday school which functions regularly in the winning of the lost will be always ready to render distinct service when a special soul-winning effort is proposed.

1. Each of the departments from the Junior up may prepare careful lists of the lost and these lists may be used as a basis for practical, intensive effort.

2. The department groups may meet daily for assignments and reports and special prayer, and may go out from these group conferences to visit and win the lost.

3. The special intensive efforts may be the proper culmination and climax of efforts regularly put forth. They will at the same time bring training and inspiration which will enable the workers in larger and more effective ways to press the regular winning efforts.

Beyond doubt, it is this persistent, systematic and intelligent effort made through the Sunday school which accounts for the great numbers of people who are now being gathered into the churches. During the ten years of largest ingathering under Charles H. Spurgeon's ministry in London, that great church received each year 364 new members. That was during the last century when the Sunday school offered no effective or extensive winning medium. During the present century, many churches are going far beyond the record made by the Tabernacle in London. The First Presbyterian Church, Seattle, Washington, has in ten years more than doubled the record of the London church. In ten years, the First

Baptist Church, Dallas, Texas, George W. Truett, pastor, has received 750 members each year. Many other churches supported by functioning Sunday schools are gathering in larger numbers than any church gathered in the last century.

THINK ON THESE THINGS:

Discuss the Sunday school as a "contact medium."

Tell of the Sunday school as a "winning medium."

"The Sunday school alone is not sufficient as a winning medium." Explain what is meant by this statement.

How did the insistence that "Miss Mary" should seek and win the lost in her class lead her to a discovery that she was not right with God?

Discuss the possibilities of the department superintendent and the general superintendent in the evangelistic program of a church.

How far do you think the practice related by Bishop Leonard of seeking to speak to at least three persons each week about salvation is practicable for believers generally?

What contribution may Cradle Roll workers make to evangelism?

What, as looking toward evangelism, may be expected of workers with Beginners and Primaries?

What, in the way of evangelism, may we expect of Junior workers?

What may we expect of Intermediate workers?

CHAPTER OUTLINE

I. A Contact Medium

II. A Winning Medium

Four factors:

1. The teacher
2. The department superintendent
3. The general superintendent
4. The pastor

III. Each of These Workers Must Stand in Line and Do His Part

IV. What May We Expect of the Departments?

V. How May the Sunday School Contribute to Special Revival Effort?

VII

USING THE BIBLE

When we come to the task of winning a soul to Christ, we do well to make use of the Word of God, the sword of the Spirit. There is no other appeal like this—pungent, powerful, convincing.

> Is not my word like a fire, saith the Lord: and like a hammer that breaketh the rock in pieces? (Jeremiah 23: 29).

> The Holy Scriptures which are able to make thee wise unto salvation through faith which is in Christ Jesus (2 Timothy 3: 15).

> Receive with meekness the engrafted word, which is able to save your souls (James 1: 21).

There are many excellent reasons for using the Word as our chief reliance.

I. WHY USE THE WORD?

1. *God promises to use and bless his Word.*

> For as the rain cometh down, and the snow from heaven, and returneth not thither, but watereth the earth, and maketh it bring forth and bud, that it may give seed to the sower, and bread to the eater; So shall my word be that goeth forth out of my mouth: it shall not return unto me void, but it shall accomplish that which I please, and it shall prosper in the thing whereto I sent it (Isaiah 55: 10, 11).

2. *God's Word produces conviction for sin.* There can be no genuine experience of grace without conviction for sin; the deeper and more real the conviction, the deeper

and more abiding are the fruits of the religious experience. It is the way of our age to think lightly concerning sin. No other words like the very words of Scripture can convince of sin.

Mr. Spurgeon relates a significant experience which illustrates the power of the Scriptures to bring conviction for sin. The great preacher's tabernacle was being remodeled and redecorated. A painter was away up in a tower on the scaffolding finishing his task. Mr. Spurgeon came into the building not knowing that any one was there. Desiring to test the acoustics of the remodeled building, he stepped to the platform and in his own impressive tones repeated John 3: 16. The words reached the ears of the painter on the scaffolding and went straight to his heart. He tried to proceed with his work, but those words of Scripture were ringing in his deepest soul. They carried conviction to his heart, and dropping his brush, the man hurried home to his Christian wife and told her what he had heard in the tabernacle. "It was a word from God," said the man, "to my soul, and I want you to pray with me that God will forgive my sins." Surely God's Word produces conviction for sin!

3. *God's Word produces faith.* "Faith cometh by hearing, and hearing by the word of God" (Romans 10: 17).

In all the ages the preaching which has produced faith has been the preaching which set forth the truth as God has revealed it in his Word. The personal testimony which has availed most has relied much on the simple Word of God. When on God's behalf we offer peace and pardon to lost men, we ought to offer these on the basis of God's own promise. When we invite and urge men to believe we ought to offer them a definite word of God on the basis of which they may believe. The writer has often used for this purpose Romans 5: 6-8:

"For when we were yet without strength, in due time Christ died for the ungodly. For scarcely for a righteous man will one die: yet peradventure for a good man some would even dare to die. But God commendeth his love

toward us, in that, while we were yet sinners, Christ died
for us." Twice over we have it here out of God's own
Word that Christ died for the ungodly. This, then, is a
sure foundation of our faith.

4. *God's Word is the means used by the Holy Spirit to
regenerate us.* This is clearly set forth in James 1: 18,
where we read: "Of his own will begat he us with the
word of truth." It is also declared in 1 Peter 1: 23: "Being born again, not of corruptible seed, but of incor-
ruptible, by the word of God, which liveth and abideth
forever."

A minister returned to the home of his boyhood to
conduct revival services. A young woman who had
grown skeptical desired, as she said afterwards, out of
sheer curiosity, to hear the man preach, whom she had
known as a boy. Shortly after she came into the church,
the preacher announced as his text Amos 4: 12, "Prepare
to meet thy God." As the text was announced and as
it was rung out again and again, the young woman began
to feel distinctly uncomfortable. As she went away from
the service her footfalls on the pavement seemed to echo
back, "Prepare to meet thy God." After she had retired,
voices out of the darkness seemed to be saying, "Prepare
to meet thy God." Unable to sleep, she arose far in the
night, procured a Bible, and in deep contrition sought
the Saviour whom she had denied and even reviled.
Surely, "the word of God is quick and powerful, and
sharper than any two-edged sword, piercing even to the
dividing asunder of soul and spirit, and of the joints and
marrow, and is a discerner of the thoughts and intents of
the heart" (Hebrews 4: 12).

In view of these facts, that God promises to use his
Word, that the Word of God convicts of sin, that it produces faith, and that it is used by the Spirit as the means
of regeneration, whoever would win souls will surely make
it his chief reliance in dealing with the lost. In thus
using the Word suffer the following suggestions:

II. How Use the Word?

1. Have the seeker to read the passage for himself. There is impressiveness and power in opening the Bible, and, after pointing out the particular passage which we wish to use, having the one with whom we deal to read perhaps aloud the words of Scripture.

2. If we quote a passage it is well to precede the words of Scripture by the reference which indicates both that it is Scripture and where it is to be found. Thus if we wish to quote the words, "Who his own self bare our sins in his body upon the tree," we should say 1 Peter 2: 24. "Who," and so forth.

3. It is well to select two or three passages on vital points, such as sin, faith and confession, and to thoroughly familiarize ourselves with these, so that we can readily turn to them and can skilfully use them. On the whole, it seems better to rely on two or three apt passages to make a given impression than to risk confusing the mind with many passages.

(1) To produce conviction for sin, use the following:

Isaiah 53: 6: "All we like sheep have gone astray; we have turned every one to his own way; and the Lord hath laid on him the iniquity of us all."

Romans 3: 10, 23: "There is none righteous, no, not one." "For all have sinned, and come short of the glory of God."

Matthew 22: 37, 38: "Jesus said unto him, Thou shalt love the Lord thy God with all thy heart, and with all thy soul, and with all thy mind. This is the first and great commandment."

Ask what is here said to be the first and great commandment. When in answer, the seeker has solemnly repeated the words of Jesus, ask him if he has done this. Show him that he owes two sets of obligations, that one goes *up* and concerns God, while the other goes *out* and concerns our fellow men. "Now, you may have fulfilled every duty to your fellows, but what of this duty which is 'first and great' to love God supremely?" Wait and press this question, praying that the Holy Spirit will send conviction.

John 3: 16. Perhaps you will wish to read it to the seeking sinner, with emphasis on the chief words. *God* so loved; God *so loved;* God so loved the *world,* including you and me; God so loved the world that *he gave his only begotten Son.* And all of this, that *whosoever believeth on him should not perish.* The love of God as expressed in the gift of his Son; the love of Jesus as shown in the gift of his life—these may be relied on to produce conviction for sin.

(2) To produce faith and bring to a decision:

Isaiah 53: 6. This verse makes the way of salvation so clear that he who runs may read. Ask the inquirer to read the first part of the verse, "All we like sheep have gone astray; we have turned every one to his own way." Stress the "all" and the "every one." Ask him if he "has gone astray" and "turned to his own way." Press the question until he is willing to admit that he is lost. Now show him in the last part of the verse what God has done with his sins, "And the Lord hath laid on him the iniquity of us all." Stress again the word "all." Remind him that the verse begins and ends with "all." Pray and wait until God's Spirit leads the seeker to see that his sins are laid on Christ and that all he needs to do is to believe this fact and to accept this Saviour.

1 Timothy 1: 15: "This is a faithful saying, and worthy of all acceptation, that Christ Jesus came into the world to save sinners; of whom I am chief." Ask the seeker, "Whom did Jesus come to save?" Hold him to this question until he says, "He came to save even the chief of sinners." "Then do you not think he is willing to save you?"

1 Peter 2: 24: "Who his own self bare our sins in his own body on the tree." Press the question, "Whose sins did Jesus bear?" When he says, "our sins," then insist that this glorious fact be at once believed and acted on.

(3) To lead in confession and baptism:

Matthew 10: 32, 33: "Whosoever therefore shall confess me before men, him will I confess also before my Father which is in heaven. But whosoever shall deny me before men, him will I also deny before my Father which is in heaven."

Romans 10: 9, 10: "That if thou shalt confess with thy mouth the Lord Jesus, and shalt believe in thine heart that God hath raised him from the dead, thou shalt be saved. For with the heart man believeth unto righteousness; and with the mouth confession is made unto salvation."

The divinely-given method of making our first great confession of Christ is the ordinance of baptism. It is well enough to sign a card, to stand up, to go forward, to confess Christ in any way; but the initial confession in which we definitely and before the world separate between the old life and the new is the act of baptism. We are then by word and work and life to confess Christ daily and hourly before the world.

THINK ON THESE THINGS:

Give some reasons for using the Word in winning to Christ.

Offer some suggestions for using the Word in winning the lost.

What Scripture would you suggest for use in producing conviction for sin?

Show how John 3: 16 may be used to produce conviction for sin.

Show how Isaiah 53: 6 may be used to lead to a decision for Christ.

What Scripture would you use to lead to public confession and baptism?

CHAPTER OUTLINE

I. Why Use the Word?

   1. God promises to bless his Word (Isaiah 55: 10, 11)

   2. God's Word produces conviction (Romans 10: 17)

   3. God's Word produces faith (Romans 10: 17)

   4. God's Word is the means used in regeneration (James 1: 18; 1 Peter 23), also used to nurture, and so forth

II. How Use the Word?

    1. Have the seeker read for himself

    2. In quoting, name chapter and verse

    3. Select and use a few vital passages

        (1) To produce conviction for sin (Isaiah 53: 6; Romans 3: 10, 23; Matthew 22: 37, 38; John 3: 16)

        (2) To produce faith (Isaiah 53: 6; 1 Timothy 1: 15; 1 Peter 2: 24)

        (3) To lead to confession (Matthew 10: 32, 33; Romans 10: 9, 10)

MEETING EXCUSES AND DIFFICULTIES

The excuses which are frequently given for staying away from Christ may not represent the real reason. The real reason why men refuse Christ, is that sin deadens and benumbs; it stills the voice of conscience. The servants in the parable of the Supper went out to call those who were bidden. "They all *with one consent* began to make excuse." Clearly there was a previous attitude of mind which accounts for the fact that they began "with one consent" to decline the invitation. The real reason was in all cases the same; they did not want to accept the invitation; they did not wish to be present at the feast. Men meet us with many excuses; we must know that back of the excuses lies the real difficulty. They do not want Christ, they do not desire to be delivered from sin. Our Lord expressed it when he said, "Ye will not come to me, that ye might have life" (John 5: 40). This strange unwillingness to come to Christ, this wilful refusal of the offers of mercy is itself the essence and evidence of sinfulness.

While this basal fact must be kept clearly in mind, it is yet helpful and necessary that we shall be able to deal with excuses as they may be made and to remove difficulties as they arise. We will especially need to know how to use the Word in dealing with the following classes:

Those who feel no conviction of sin, and hence have no desire to be saved.

Those who, convicted of sin, are anxious to be saved, but have difficulties.

Those who, convicted of sin, are anxious to be saved, but are ignorant of the way of life.

Those who are beset with doubts.

I. Those Who Have No Conviction of Sin, and Hence Have No Desire to Be Saved

This will constitute by far the largest number of the lost with whom we shall deal. They feel no concern for their spiritual condition; they meet all of our approaches and our solicitude with cool indifference; they would be let alone. What is to be our attitude toward these who have no interest in our Lord and no concern about the eternal life which he offers?

1. *We are not to let them alone*

This is their desire, to be left alone, as it is our temptation. They would fain be left alone in their ease of conscience and in their indulgence of sin. They would have us think indeed that our efforts and our concern only drive them farther away. Some country youths in Kentucky were making their way home near midnight. They saw lying by the roadside a little mound covered with snow. Pushing back the snow, they discovered to their amazement the body of a man; a neighbor had fallen in a drunken stupor and was now in evident peril of freezing to death. The young men took in the situation in a moment, and realizing the man's peril, resolved to carry him safely home. But the man pleaded to be let alone, and when his pleas were unavailing, he resisted, cursing bitterly and fighting with all his might. The stalwart youths, one under either arm and one behind, marched the man down the road and never left him until they saw him safe in his own home.

Our lost friends wish to be left alone; above all things they would have us leave them undisturbed. But to leave them alone may mean eternal death.

2. *We are to use such Scripture passages as will convince them of sin.*

(1) Use James 2: 10: "For whosoever shall keep the whole law, and yet offend in one point, he is guilty of all."

There is unity in the divine law; broken in one point it is broken in all. If a man be suspended by a chain of ten links, and one of these links shall break, the man falls as surely as if every link had broken at the same time. Ask the lost one to read slowly these words of James 2: 10. Then ask him if he has not "offended in one point.

(2) Use Hebrews 10: 28, 29: "He that despised Moses' law died without mercy under two or three witnesses: Of how much sorer punishment, suppose ye, shall he be thought worthy, who hath trodden under foot the Son of God, and hath counted the blood of the covenant, where-with he was sanctified, an unholy thing, and hath done despite unto the Spirit of grace?"

Show the one whom you seek to win that to reject Christ is the greatest of sins. Ask him if he knows that in refusing Christ he has "trodden under foot the Son of God?" Let him read for himself, that he hath counted the blood of the covenant an unholy thing and hath done despite unto the Spirit of grace. Wait and pray till the Spirit bears in on the soul a conviction of sin, for we may be well assured that without conviction of sin there can be no remission.

II. THOSE WHO, CONVICTED OF SIN, ARE ANXIOUS TO BE SAVED, BUT HAVE DIFFICULTIES

This is a more hopeful state. When a sense of sin has been aroused and there is even the slightest desire to be saved, our task is definite and clear. We are, with the help of the Holy Spirit, to hasten to remove the barriers which stand in the way of surrender and faith. Note some of the difficulties which we are sure to encounter:

1. *"I am too great a sinner; God cannot save me."*

If one makes this statement with any semblance of sincerity, there is hope for his early conversion; he is "not far from the Kingdom." At first Satan makes us believe that we are good enough to be saved without

Christ; later he would persuade us that we are so bad that even Christ cannot save us.

(1) Use Luke 19: 10: "For the Son of man is come to seek and to save that which was lost."

Why did the Son of man come? Who is it Christ came to seek and to save? Press these questions until the sinner answers them for himself. If a trained surgeon comes into a group of men, some of whom are in perfect physical condition and some of whom are maimed and crippled, which class of these men will most attract the eye and heart of the surgeon?

(2) Use also 1 Timothy 1: 15: "This is a faithful saying, and worthy of all acceptation, that Christ Jesus came into the world to save sinners; of whom I am chief."

A man, who had led a life of dissipation, and who had only recently been separated from his wife said to a Christian minister, in response to his question, why he was not a Christian, "I am too great a sinner to be saved." The minister turned to 1 Timothy 1: 15. The man said, "Well, I am the chief of sinners." "Then," said the preacher, "that verse means you." The man replied, "It is a precious promise." Asked, "Will you accept it now?" he said firmly, "I will." Desiring to confirm his faith and seal his acceptance of the Saviour, the minister said, "Let us kneel down and tell God so." The two knelt together and the man confessed to God his sins and asked God for Christ's sake to forgive him his sins. Asked again if he really accepted Christ, he said he did. Asked if he really believed he was saved, he declared that he did. At the first opportunity the man confessed Christ. The minister was able to follow him when he removed to another city. The man became an active Christian, making place in his life for many forms of Christian service. He sought a reunion with his wife, adopted a little child from an orphans' home and came to have a happy Christian home.

2. *"I have no feeling."*

Many people find difficulty in that though they wish to be saved, they do not experience the feeling which they somehow expect.

(1) Show this class that God's order is "fact, faith, and feeling." They err in that they seek to put feeling first. Lead them to see that God begins with fact, that he puts faith second and that feeling properly comes after fact and faith.

Fact. God begins with facts. It is a fact that God loves sinful men. It is a fact that in due time Christ died for the ungodly. It is a fact that salvation is offered on the basis of unconditional surrender and childlike trust. These are facts and with them we do well to begin. Ponder them well.

Faith. God next asks faith. "Believe in the Lord Jesus Christ and thou shalt be saved." We believe, we exercise faith. We accept Christ as a personal Saviour and trust him for salvation.

Feeling. When by faith we plant ourselves on the fact of Christ's atoning merit and have been forgiven, then comes feeling, the feeling of joy and love and gratitude. This clearly is God's order.

Alas that the sinner in his blindness and self-conceit should wish to reverse this order and should expect and demand feeling first and refuse to exercise faith until God has given feeling!

(2) Use Isaiah 55: 7: "Let the wicked forsake his way and the unrighteous man his thoughts: and let him return unto the Lord, and he will have mercy upon him; and to our God, for he will abundantly pardon."

God demands that the sinner *shall forsake his way.* He does not require that the sinner shall have certain feelings. In no other department of life or duty do we wait for feeling.

3. *"There is some one whom I cannot forgive."*

(1) Show them that they must forgive. To foster the spirit of resentment is to harbor fires in the heart which

will burn and destroy. Our hatred of another does not necessarily injure that other, but it does necessarily and greatly injure ourselves. This yielding to resentment so far from indicating strength is born of weakness. It is a flaming fire, an eating cancer, a deadly virus. We *must* forgive, whether or not we care to become Christians. ✦

(2) Show them that they *can* forgive. Indeed, when one says, "I cannot forgive," he would better say, "I will not forgive." Besides, what we cannot do unaided and in our own strength, we can easily do with the help of God's Holy Spirit. "I can do all things through Christ which strengtheneth me."

(3) God cannot forgive us our sins except we forgive those who sin against us.

Use Mark 11: 25, 26: "And when ye stand praying, forgive, if ye have ought against any: that your Father also which is in heaven may forgive you your trespasses. But if ye do not forgive, neither will your Father which is in heaven forgive you your trespasses."

4. *"I fear I cannot hold out."*

(1) Use 2 Timothy 1: 12: "For I know whom I have believed, and am persuaded that he is able to keep that which I have committed unto him against that day."

Christ assumes responsibility for our keeping; we are not any longer to keep ourselves. The headlight of the great locomotive engine throws its light only a few hundred yards ahead; as the engine drives forward in the darkness, the light keeps well ahead. It would be a foolish engineer who would sit down and demand that light be flashed all the way to his destination. Ask the sinner to accept Christ and walk out with him, trusting that light and help will be given for every emergency.

(2) Use also Jude 24: "Now unto him that is able to keep you from falling, and to present you faultless before the presence of his glory with exceeding joy."

5. *"There are too many hypocrites in the church."*

Use Acts 16: 31: "Believe on the Lord Jesus Christ, and thou shalt be saved." Call this excuse-maker to face the real issue. He is not asked to believe on the friends of Jesus. He is asked to believe *on Jesus* as Lord and Saviour. The real issue is not between him and the professed followers of the Lord. The issue is between him and the Lord himself. The searching question for every lost soul is: "What think ye of Christ, whose son is he?" The issue which cannot be avoided is, "What will ye do with Jesus, which is called Christ?" Hold the objector to this issue. Show him that it is mere child's play to refuse Christ, to deny his just claims, because forsooth, some professed friends of Jesus are inconsistent in their profession. Some pretended followers of Jesus are unworthy. Jesus himself is worthy. Men are asked to believe on Jesus, not on the followers of Jesus.

If these objectors really wish to avoid association with hypocrites, they should accept Jesus as Lord and live for him in his church; else they must live with hypocrites here and spend eternity with them.

III. THOSE WHO, CONVICTED OF SIN, ARE ANXIOUS TO BE SAVED, BUT DO NOT KNOW THE PLAN OF SALVATION

These are not difficult to deal with. The three Scriptures discussed in the last chapter under *bringing to a decision* may be used here:

1. *God offers salvation upon two conditions:*

(1) *Repentance.* Show that what God requires first of every sinner is that he shall repent.

Luke 13: 3: "Except ye repent, ye shall all likewise perish."

Three things are involved in the duty to repent: (a) a new thought, a new view of sin; (b) a new feeling toward sin, a recognition of its heinousness in God's sight; (c) a new attitude toward sin, a turning from it.

Stated in simpler fashion, (a) Repentance is not sorrow for sin. It involves sorrow for sin and there can be no repentance without such sorrow, but it is not merely sorrow for sin; (b) Repentance certainly is not remorse for sin. Judas was smitten with remorse, but instead of seeking the Saviour whom he had betrayed, he went out and hanged himself; (c) Repentance is being sorry enough for sin to renounce it and forsake it, and turn to Christ for pardon.

(2) *Faith*. John 1: 12: "But as many as received him, to them gave he power to become the sons of God, even to them that believe on his name."

A woman once came to me in great agitation. After many ineffectual attempts she was at last able to unburden her heart. Fourteen years before she had killed a man, and had borne the memory of the act upon her conscience until it had almost driven her crazy. When she told the story to another Christian and myself, we turned to Isaiah 53: 6. After reading the verse very carefully to her, I asked her what the Lord had done with her sin. After a few minutes' deep and anxious thought, she said, "He has laid it on Christ." I took a book in my hand. "Now," I said, "let my right hand represent you and my left hand Christ, and this book your sin." I laid the book upon my right hand and I said, "Where is your sin now?" She said, "On me." "Now," I said, "What has God done with it?" She said, "Laid it on Christ," and I laid the book over on the other hand. "Where is your sin now?" I asked. It was long before she could summon courage to answer, and then with a desperate effort, she said, "On Christ." I said, "Then is it on you any longer?" Slowly the light came into her face and she burst out with a cry, "No," it is on him, it is on Christ."—R. A. Torrey, in *How to Bring Men to Christ.*

2. *God requires as evidence of this salvation and in grati-*
tude for it:

(1) That we *confess* Christ before the world. Romans
10: 9, 10: "That if thou shalt confess with thy mouth
the Lord Jesus, and shalt believe in thine heart that
God hath raised him from the dead, thou shalt be saved.
For with the heart man believeth unto righteousness;
and with the mouth confession is made unto salvation."

(2) That we accept Christ as *Lord of our lives.* Acts
2: 36: "Therefore let all the house of Israel know as-
suredly, that God hath made that same Jesus whom ye
have crucified, both Lord and Christ."

(3) That we *work out* our salvation. Philippians 2:
12, 13: "Wherefore, my beloved, as ye have always
obeyed, not as in my presence only, but now much more
in my absence, work out your own salvation with fear
and trembling. For it is God which worketh in you
both to will and to do of his good pleasure."

Christ is to be Lord as well as Saviour. He is to be
the arbiter of our conduct and henceforth our duty is to
serve him. We are saved that we may save and serve.

IV. THOSE WHO ARE BESET WITH DOUBTS

Here we may encounter two classes: those who doubt
God and his revelation in general, and those who in
particular doubt their own acceptance with the Lord.

1. *Those who doubt God and his revelation.*

Only occasionally, perhaps, will we be called to deal
with confirmed and hardened doubters. Frequently we
may be called to deal with youths who dare to challenge
God and the verity of his Word.

(1) Usually they are not to be argued with. Argu-
ment at this time is more likely to confirm than to
convince. A young girl came to Miss Margaret Slattery,
telling her of her doubts, deep and grave doubts, about
the most vital things in religion, including the very
existence of God. Miss Slattery did not argue. She said

very quietly, "Tell me some things you do believe. Do you believe that Jesus was good and true?" Quick came the reply, "I have never questioned that; he was the best and the truest man this world ever saw and he is the world's greatest teacher." "Then," said Miss Slattery, "believe Jesus as far as you can. Read his word, obey his teaching and he will give you light." The question rested there. The wise teacher sent the doubting girl away with her feet resting securely on certain ground which she could accept and from which she could pass on to larger faith.

(2) Positive teaching may answer negative questions. Some one tells of a missionary who sought to guide and help a brilliant young Chinese student who was beset with doubts. He doubted the miracles, special providences, and other New Testament teachings; he laid his doubts before his missionary friend. The missionary said, "Perhaps we are beginning at the wrong end. Is there nothing in the New Testament which you can believe?" The Chinaman declared that there was much of beauty and truth about which he could raise no question. "Now," said the missionary, "read your New Testament carefully, underscoring everything that you can believe, and when I come this way again, we will talk these things over." The young student began his reading and his underscoring. He was surprised and pleased to see how much he could believe. As he proceeded, his beliefs grew and faith swept away his doubts. When the missionary returned, he found his young friend resting happily in assured peace.

2. *Those who doubt their own acceptance with the Lord.*

A particular phase of doubt with which Christian workers are frequently called to deal concerns *the question of personal acceptance with the Lord.*

(1) This kind of doubt may grow out of *the habit of introspection.* Young people are prone to look much within, to consider unduly their frames and feelings. In

the matter of our personal salvation, scant comfort can come from looking within. The basis of our hope, the ground of our assurance, lies not within us, in any merit. or any feelings or experience of our own. Such basis is in the love of God, in the atonement of Jesus, and the promise of God which standeth sure. Assurance of faith will come to the youthful believer as he learns to look away from himself, to give over the habit of introspection and to rely upon the unchangeable love and promise of the Lord.

(2) Such doubt may come of *comparing our religious experience with* the experiences of other people. In experience meetings and love feasts, young Christians hear the wonderful dealings of God with others and the striking experiences through which others have come, and because, forsooth, there were not given to them visions so clear and joys so marked, they are tempted to question whether theirs is a genuine experience.

Similarly there are not wanting those who set up before themselves some ideal religious experience, and by comparing their own with this, force themselves into doubt. We have no Scripture warrant for hanging our faith on any type of experience. The faith which saves is the faith which sees Christ as the sufficient atoning Saviour.

(3) Doubt of our acceptance with the Lord may result from the *doing of doubtful things*. Whoever does doubtful things will doubt. If we insist upon living close upon the border-line between the church and the world, if we persist in going as far as we dare toward the things of the old life, we may not be surprised if at times we find ourselves in doubt as to which side of the line we are really on.

A bit of incident is related as occurring in Bristol, Tennessee-Virginia. The city lies on the border between the two states, the state line running down the main street of the city. A big sheriff on the Virginia side undertook to arrest a man for some misdemeanor. The man slipped across the state line and, safely out of the sheriff's jurisdiction, turned to laugh at the expense of the big sheriff. The officer was equal to the occasion; assuming a friendly air, he said, "Joe, old fellow, I was wrong to think of arresting you for so small a matter. Shake hands and let's be friends!" Caught completely off his guard, the man walked up to the sheriff and clasped his hand. Instantly the sheriff's hand closed like a vise; there was a brief struggle, and the sheriff safely landed his man. If we play tag with Satan across the boundary line we are almost sure to be landed into the camp of his Satanic Majesty. If we do not go so far we must at least be disturbed and beset with doubt as to whether we really belong in the camps of the Lord.

(4) Such doubt may come of *idleness in the Kingdom.* Joyful assurance is impossible to us if we are not engaged in the things of the Master. The only sure proof that we are followers of Jesus lies in the fact that we are actually following him; the best evidence that we are servants of the Lord lies in the fact that we are actually serving him.

> There's no other way
> To be happy in Jesus
> But to trust and obey.

A young man came to his pastor and said: "I give it up; I think I was never converted. I wish you would have my name stricken from the church roll." The wise pastor replied, "Very well, we will see about that. Meantime, this is a busy day with me. I want you to help me. I was going to take this basket of groceries to Widow C——, but I am called away on another mission. Will you go for me?" Certainly, he would go. "But what that widow and those children need more than the groceries is a vision of God and a message from his Word. I want you to take this Testament and read and pray in that home." The youth protested, declaring that he had never done such a thing. The pastor replied, "They are poor and unlearned; you can easily render this service. Promise me that you will read and pray with them. I cannot let you take the groceries unless you will do so." The promise was reluctantly made. The boy's heart was touched to see the joy of the widow and the gladness of the children as they opened the basket. He said blushingly, "I promised the pastor I would read and pray. If the children will sit down I will do the best I can."

He read about the Father's house where the many mansions are. As he read his eye stole a furtive glance around the poor, bare room, and the word of Jesus about the mansions seemed sweeter than ever before. Then they knelt to pray, and while the young man poured out his heart in prayer, the angels seemed to be hovering near. The young man walked out of that home with a sense of God's presence and goodness which he had never felt before. Meeting the pastor later in the day, the youth who had lost assurance and had decided to drop out of the church, made report: "Pastor, I did what I promised; I read and prayed in that home and the Lord blessed me. When you want any more groceries delivered to a home like that, call on me. And, pastor, you need not say anything for the present about taking my name off the church book."

Put the doubter to work; give him some serious task for the Lord and for his fellows. When the doubter gets to work and warms to his task he ceases to doubt. These young Christians long to serve; they are in the restless, energetic age. Scarcely any crime against them is greater than to leave them idle when they so desire to serve and when their service is so greatly needed. Alas, that so often these restless, energetic spirits are left without suitable tasks!

THINK ON THESE THINGS:

How may we deal helpfully with one who has no conviction of sin and hence no desire to be saved?

How may we help one who feels that he is so great a sinner that God cannot save him?

What instruction may we give to one who says, "I have no feeling"?

What help may we offer one who harbors an unforgiving spirit?

What guidance may be offered one who wishes to be saved, but does not know the way of salvation?

What does God require as evidence of salvation and in gratitude for it?

CHAPTER OUTLINE

I. Those Who Have No Conviction of Sin
   1. Not to let them alone
   2. Use appropriate Scriptures (James 2: 10; Hebrews 10: 28, 29)

II. Those Who Have Difficulties
   1. "I am too great a sinner" (Luke 19: 10; 1 Timothy 1: 15)
   2. "I have no feeling"
   3. "There is some one I cannot forgive"
   4. "I fear I cannot hold out" (2 Timothy 1: 12; Jude 24)
   5. "There are too many hypocrites in the churches" (Acts 16: 31)

III. Those Who, Convicted of Sin, Do Not Know the Plan of Salvation
   1. Conditions are two
      (1) Repentance
      (2) Faith
   2. God requires as evidence of salvation
      (1) That we confess Christ
      (2) That we accept Christ as Lord
      (3) That we "work out" our salvation

IV. Those Who Are Beset with Doubts
   1. Those who doubt God and his revelation
   2. Those who doubt their own acceptance with the Lord

HOW TO MAKE A SUCCESS OF THE CHRISTIAN LIFE

When we have brought a lost soul to trust Jesus as Saviour, our next concern must be so to guide and instruct the new believer as to help him to make a success in the venture upon which he has entered. All of the people who make a beginning in the Christian life quickly fall into two classes; one class makes a partial or complete failure in the undertaking, while the other class makes a complete success in the effort to live the Christian way. But why should there be failures? Is it not incumbent upon us who win to Christ to offer such simple and faithful guidance as may, under the Holy Spirit, lead on to success?

We offer suggestions along three lines:

I. SOME INITIAL SUGGESTIONS

Where so much is at stake, very naturally many minds would lend themselves to the effort to make a concise statement and offer definite suggestions to the Christian beginner. A generation ago that careful evangelist, R. A. Torrey, issued a tract bearing the title, "How to Make a Success of the Christian Life." Among other suggestions, this widely-circulated leaflet contained five which are here condensed:

1. *Begin Right.* Jesus tells us of the right beginning, John 1: 12: "But as many as received him, to them gave he power to become the sons of God, even to them that believe on his name." Receive Christ. Take him as your Saviour who died for your sins. Trust the whole matter of your forgiveness to him. Rest upon the fact that he paid the full penalty of your sins. It is in this first step

that many make a mistake. They try to mix in their good works as a ground of salvation. Take him as your deliverer, the one who will save you from the power of sin. Don't try to save yourself from the power of sin. Trust him to do it. Take him as your Master. Don't seek to guide your own life. Surrender unconditionally to him. Say "All for Jesus." If you wish to make a success of the Christian life, go alone with God; get down on your knees and say "All for Jesus." Say it very earnestly; say it from your heart. Stay there until you realize what it means and what you are doing.

2. *Confess Christ Openly Before Men.* Matthew 10: 32: "Whosoever therefore shall confess me before men, him will I confess before my Father which is in heaven." This does not mean that we are to confess Christ just once, as for example when we unite with the church, but constantly. If you would make a success of the Christian life, seize every opportunity of confessing Christ before men—in the home, in shopping, at work, in the church, everywhere. How many have fallen away from Christ at this point! They went to a new city or a new place to work, and neglected to confess Christ, and now they are back in the world.

3. *Go To Work for Christ.* The working Christian, the one who uses his talents, whether few or many, in Christ's service, is the one who gets on in the Christian life here, and who will hereafter hear the "Well done, thou good and faithful servant, enter thou into the joy of thy Lord." Find some work to do for Christ and do it. Seek for work. If it is nothing more than distributing tracts or invitations to meeting, do it. Always be looking for something more to do for Christ, and you will always be receiving something more from Christ.

4. *Give Largely.* "The liberal soul shall be made fat." Success and growth in the Christian life depend upon few things more than upon liberal giving. A stingy Christian cannot be a growing Christian. It is wonderful how a Christian begins to grow when he begins to

give. Give systematically. Set aside for God a fixed proportion of all the money or goods you get. Be exact and honest about it. A tenth is a good proportion to begin with. Don't let it be less than that. After you have given your tenth you will soon learn the joy of giving free-will offerings in addition to the tenth.

5. *Keep Right On.* Forget that which lies behind, press on to that which lies before. Forget the sins which lie behind. If you fail anywhere, if you fall, don't be discouraged, don't give up, don't brood over the sin. Confess it instantly. Believe the sin is forgiven, press on. If he can, Satan will keep you brooding over your sins and failures.

Forget the achievements and victories of the past, and press on to greater things. Here Satan cheats many of us out of the larger life. I have seen this in many individuals and many churches. "How well we have done!" they think. Our only safety is in forgetting those things which are behind and pressing on. Press on, there is always something better ahead.

II. READ THE BIBLE AND PRAY DAILY

1. *Read the Bible.* Read deliberately and meditatively some portion of the Scriptures each day. Do this persistently and without fail. Many believers find it helpful to keep a book of hymns along with the Bible and to read one or more hymns during each devotional season.

2. *Pray.* Persist in prayer until conscious of the Father's presence and blessing.

The following is perhaps a normal order of prayer, though the leadings of the Spirit and our own impulse will vary it indefinitely:

(1) *Invocation.* Humbly entreat God to lend a listening ear, and mercifully to grant his presence in the secret place.

(2) *Adoration.* Still the heart and, with or without words, adore God. Ponder his perfection, meditate upon his attributes, think upon his goodness.

(3) *Thanksgiving.* Name over, perhaps write down, some of the things for which your heart is grateful. Let your heart be all aglow with glad gratitude.

(4) *Confession.* Think deep into your heart-life. Call up and confess to the Father your short-comings and sins.

(5) *Petition.* Present at a throne of mercy your conscious needs, among which will probably be (a) daily bread, (b) strength equal to your need, (c) gentleness of temper and sweetness of spirit, (d) unselfishness of heart, (e) kindly and merciful speech, (f) quietness and confidence before the Lord.

(6) *Intercession.* Pray for others; that is a poor hour of prayer which does not secure blessing for others as well as ourselves. For whom shall we pray?

a. Each one in our home and family circle.

b. Not these alone, but the town and country in which we live.

c. The pastor, the officers, and members of our church.

d. The superintendent, teachers and pupils of our Sunday school.

e. The leaders and members of any special department in which we work.

f. The sick, the sorrowing, the aged. Call them up and present them to the Father by name.

g. The wayward, the tempted, all who are in any way grieving the Lord.

h. All the departments of denominational life.

(a) The orphans' home which we are accustomed to support with our gifts and prayers.

(b) The hospital or hospitals in which we are particularly interested.

(c) The mission work in both home and foreign fields.

(d) The state paper.

(e) The Christian schools and seminaries.

"Confess therefore your sins one to another, and pray one for another, that ye may be healed. The supplication of a righteous man availeth much in its working" (James 5: 16 ASV).

The reader may wish to copy this order of prayer and paste it in his Bible for daily use.

III. Distinguish Sharply Between Right and Wrong

The Christian life is a ceaseless battle between right on the one hand and wrong on the other hand. Here we raise three questions:

1. *What is right?*

Is there essential difference between right and wrong? Everywhere old landmarks are being removed; conventions are broken down; distinctions between right and wrong are obscured.

This condition is not wholly or distinctly modern. Hundreds of years before Christ came to the earth the prophet, Isaiah, denounced those who obscured right and wrong, who broke down conventions and who sought to remove old landmarks; "woe unto them that call evil good, and good evil; that put darkness for light, and light for darkness; that put bitter for sweet, and sweet for bitter" (Isaiah 5: 20).

(1) Right is right, and wrong is wrong. They differ in their origin, they differ in their genius, they differ in the direction in which they go. Long ago, the English poet sang,

> East is East and
> West is West and
> Ne'er the twain shall meet.

We may say with equal propriety, "Right is right and wrong is wrong. And ne'er the twain shall meet." They cannot meet. They come from different directions and they tend in different directions.

(2) Right emanates from God. Right reflects God. Right is right because—God. Wrong emanates from Satan. Wrong reflects Satan. Between right and wrong is a great gulf fixed and impassable.

(3) Right creates; wrong destroys. Right builds up; wrong pulls down. Right is essentially and always creative and constructive; wrong is inevitably and always destructive. Right pays; wrong never pays. Right is profitable, it satisfies; wrong is never profitable, it never really satisfies.

2. *How are we to know right from wrong?*

This is not so simple as it may at first appear. In a world of confusion, of mixed ideals, of conflicting teachings, how are we to know right from wrong?

(1) We answer the question negatively:

a. We cannot safely follow moral and spiritual labels. In our day, as in Isaiah's day, the labels are sadly mxeid. Men are calling good evil and evil good. The housewife may safely follow the labels on foods and drugs; the pure-food laws offer protection here. The driver on the state and national highways may safely follow the highway signs. But in our moral and spiritual living we cannot follow the signs. The labels are mixed; the signs are misplaced and confused.

b. *We dare not follow custom.* Our problem would be greatly simplified if we could follow custom; but custom changes. Custom merely reflects moral and spiritual ideals at a given time and within certain areas. Dead fish drift with the currents. Only live fish have the instinct and ability to go against the currents.

c. *We cannot safely follow conscience.* Let us think clearly here. Conscience is given, not primarily to tell us what is right, but rather to tell us to do the right. Conscience, if one is misguided as to right, may lead to do wrong. A company of bandits, their hands red with blood, sat down on Friday to a table on which

meat was offered. After they had begun to eat the meat,
some one suggested that the day was Friday. Instantly
the men grew pale, pushed back the meat and refused
to partake of it. Their consciences permitted them to rob
and murder, but forbade them to eat meat on Friday!
Conscience itself must be enlightened. Conscience can
only tell us to do what we think is right. Conscience
cannot always be depended on to tell us the difference
between right and wrong.

(2) We answer our question positively:

Space permits only some brief proposals.

a. If one is in doubt as to the right or wrong of a given
attitude or course of action, he may well make that attitude or course of action objective. So long as it remains
subjective, hidden away in his own heart, he will look at
it through rose-colored glasses. He must lift it out of
himself, separate it from himself, make it objective, in
order to see it in its proper light. Once the problem
becomes thus objective, it may be easy to determine its
moral quality.

Take, for example, the series of deadly sins into which
David fell. David had passed through strenuous days.
In an evil hour he had indulged sin, and sin had led
on to deeper sin. Somehow David looked upon these
sins through indulgent eyes. He failed to see the enormity
of the crimes into which he had fallen. God sent Nathan,
the prophet, to reveal to him his sins. Nathan proceeded
to lift David's sins from the subjective to the objective.
He told a simple story, a parable, in which he sought to
picture the king to himself. It was an exact picture of
David's evil course. The king failed to recognize his
own likeness. In anger he swore that the man thus black
with guilt should die. Then Nathan said to David,
"Thou art the man." All at once David's sin flashed
upon him. Repentance, deep and terrible, followed. It
will often help us to know what is right if we can lift
a given problem out of the subjective and look at it
objectively.

b. Where doubt exists as to right and wrong, one may "orient" the problem and thus see it in better perspective. Thus one may project oneself to a later period in life and see how with the added and enlarged experience the particular problem will be viewed. If one is twenty he may imagine himself thirty or forty and raise a question as to how this course of action will appear in the larger maturity of the later day. If one finds difficulty in thus orienting oneself it is always possible to sit down with some trusted friend who has attained the fuller experience and ask that friend to discuss the moral quality of a given attitude or course of procedure.

c. In case of doubt as to right or wrong one may re-incarnate a given procedure. Let him transfer from himself to a trusted and honored friend the case in question. How would this attitude or this procedure appear in this trusted friend? What would be his reaction if he knew that his honored friend was doing this thing about which he is in doubt? A certain man who greatly admired Mahatma Ghandi formed the habit, when in doubt, of saying, "What would Ghandi do?" We, of course, have one greater than Ghandi whom we can regard as our exemplar. What would Jesus do, is always a safe and helpful question.

d. We may universalize a given conduct and thus determine whether it is right or wrong. What if every other person should do this thing or pursue this course? Whatever is right for me is under the same conditions right for every other man. Right knows no partialities and plays no favorites. Whoever wishes to be right must be rigid and exacting with himself.

e. The Bible must of course be our dependable guide as to right and wrong. We will need to use the Holy Scriptures with discretion. The Bible does not offer a code of laws for our specific guidance. It is not a blueprint to be slavishly followed. It is not a highway map which we can follow in the moral and spiritual realm as we would follow the highway map in making a journey.

In its own way the Bible brings light on our pathway and offers solution for our problems.

3. *How are we to find power to do the right which we know?*

Here, after all, is our chiefest problem. Generally speaking we can know what is right, but how are we to find strength to do the right? Paul spoke for us all: "For that which I do I know not: for not what I would, that do I practise; but what I hate, that I do. But if what I would not, that I do, I consent unto the law that it is good. So now it is no more I that do it, but sin which dwelleth in me" (Romans 7: 15-17 RV).

The age-long conflict of the two natures which struggle within every believer is clearly set forth in the story of "Big Bill Thompson." Big Bill was the college athlete. He was as hard as adamant. And yet the men felt that in Bill there were two men. There was another spirit in Bill. On another side of his nature he was singularly gentle and generous. One day Big Bill and "Joe," his pal, were talking together on the campus. Joe said:

"Bill, they say that you are a mystery. You are two men. We don't understand you. There are experiences in your life which you have not chosen to tell us. Now, Bill, I do not seek your confidence, but if ever you want to tell your life story to anybody, I want you to know you can trust me."

Big Bill sprang to his feet: "Joe, there will never be a better time than now."

He strode away across the campus, Joe following him. Neither spoke a word. Into the dormitory Bill led and down the hall, to his own room; Joe followed. Bill walked across the room and paused in front of a woman's picture. It seemed too young to be Bill's mother. It appeared too old to be Bill's sweetheart. Bill told his own story:

"Joe, it's my mother. I never saw her. I get the story from my father. When I was born, something occurred which was not on the schedule. The good physician walked into the next room where my father sat and said, "Mr. Thompson, I can save only one life. You must decide. Shall it be the mother or the child?"

Quickly the man said what any man would have said under the circumstances: "Why, save the mother, of course." Just then the mother's voice was heard from the next room. The doctor responded. She said, "Call my husband." The two men stood before her. "Doctor, I heard what you said. I know what it means. Now that question is for me to decide. Doctor, you are to save the child." The physician looked to Mr. Thompson for a final word. "Doctor," he said, "she is right. It is hers to decide. She has decided. You are to save the child."

"Joe," Bill said, "I am here because she is not. I enjoy this wide beautiful world because she went down into a dark narrow grave."

Bill continued: "Joe, the men are right. I am two men. Two men struggle within me. *She* lives within me. God alone knows how I long to be like her and how I long to reproduce her. Then there is another nature within me. They war, the one against the other."

It is even so, with every believer. On and on, the battle must continue. "For the good which I would I do not: but the evil which I would not, that I practise" (Romans 7: 19 ASV). Paul's hope of ultimate triumph is our hope of ultimate triumph; "Wretched man that I am! who shall deliver me out of the body of this death? I thank God through Jesus Christ our Lord. So then I of myself with the mind, indeed, serve the law of God; but with the flesh of the law of sin" (Romans 7: 24, 25 ASV).

THINK ON THESE THINGS:

What initial suggestions would you make to one who wants to
  make a success of the Christian life?
What would you suggest about Bible reading and prayer?
What is the normal order of prayer?
How would you distinguish between right and wrong?
Is conscience a safe guide?
Can we follow custom?
Where can we find power to do right when we know it?

CHAPTER OUTLINE

I. Some Initial Suggestions
  1. Begin right
  2. Confess Christ openly before men
  3. Go to work for Christ
  4. Give largely
  5. Keep right on

II. Read the Bible and Pray Daily
  1. Read the Bible
  2. Pray
    (1) Invocation
    (2) Adoration
    (3) Thanksgiving
    (4) Confession
    (5) Petition
    (6) Intercession

III. Distinguish Sharply Between Right and Wrong?
    1. What is right?
    2. How are we to know right from wrong?
    3. How are we to find power to do the right which we know?